T0301966

An Analysis of

Samuel P. Huntington's

The Clash of Civilizations and the Remaking of World Order

Riley Quinn

Published by Macat International Ltd
24:13 Coda Centre, 189 Munster Road, London SW6 6AW.

Distributed exclusively by Routledge
2 Park Square, Milton Park, Abingdon, Oxon OX14 4RN
711 Third Avenue, New York, NY 10017, USA

Routledge is an imprint of the Taylor & Francis Group, an informa business

www.macat.com
info@macat.com

Cataloguing in Publication Data
A catalogue record for this book is available from the British Library.
Library of Congress Cataloguing-in-Publication Data is available upon request.
Cover illustration: Etienne Gilfillan

ISBN 978-1-912303-30-4 (hardback)
ISBN 978-1-912127-92-4 (paperback)
ISBN 978-1-912282-18-0 (e-book)

Notice
The information in this book is designed to orientate readers of the work under analysis,
to elucidate and contextualise its key ideas and themes, and to aid in the development
of critical thinking skills. It is not meant to be used, nor should it be used, as a
substitute for original thinking or in place of original writing or research. References and
notes are provided for informational purposes and their presence does not constitute
endorsement of the information or opinions therein. This book is presented solely for
educational purposes. It is sold on the understanding that the publisher is not engaged
to provide any scholarly advice. The publisher has made every effort to ensure that
this book is accurate and up-to-date, but makes no warranties or representations with
regard to the completeness or reliability of the information it contains. The information
and the opinions provided herein are not guaranteed or warranted to produce particular
results and may not be suitable for students of every ability. The publisher shall not be
liable for any loss, damage or disruption arising from any errors or omissions, or from
the use of this book, including, but not limited to, special, incidental, consequential or
other damages caused, or alleged to have been caused, directly or indirectly, by the
information contained within.

CONTENTS

THE MACAT LIBRARY

The Macat Library is a series of unique academic explorations of seminal works in the humanities and social sciences – books and papers that have had a significant and widely recognised impact on their disciplines. It has been created to serve as much more than just a summary of what lies between the covers of a great book. It illuminates and explores the influences on, ideas of, and impact of that book. Our goal is to offer a learning resource that encourages critical thinking and fosters a better, deeper understanding of important ideas.

Each publication is divided into three Sections: Influences, Ideas, and Impact. Each Section has four Modules. These explore every important facet of the work, and the responses to it.

This Section-Module structure makes a Macat Library book easy to use, but it has another important feature. Because each Macat book is written to the same format, it is possible (and encouraged!) to cross-reference multiple Macat books along the same lines of inquiry or research. This allows the reader to open up interesting interdisciplinary pathways.

To further aid your reading, lists of glossary terms and people mentioned are included at the end of this book (these are indicated by an asterisk [*] throughout) – as well as a list of works cited.

Macat has worked with the University of Cambridge to identify the elements of critical thinking and understand the ways in which six different skills combine to enable effective thinking.
Three allow us to fully understand a problem; three more give us the tools to solve it. Together, these six skills make up the **PACIER** model of critical thinking. They are:

ANALYSIS – understanding how an argument is built
EVALUATION – exploring the strengths and weaknesses of an argument
INTERPRETATION – understanding issues of meaning

CREATIVE THINKING – coming up with new ideas and fresh connections
PROBLEM-SOLVING – producing strong solutions
REASONING – creating strong arguments

To find out more, visit **WWW.MACAT.COM.**

CRITICAL THINKING AND *THE CLASH OF CIVILIZATIONS*

Primary critical thinking skill: PROBLEM-SOLVING
Secondary critical thinking skill: INTERPRETATION

The end of the Cold War, which occurred early in the 1990s, brought joy and freedom to millions. But it posed a difficult question to the world's governments and to the academics who studied them: how would world order be remade in an age no longer dominated by the competing ideologies of capitalism and communism?

Samuel P. Huntington was one of the many political scientists who responded to this challenge by conceiving works that attempted to predict the ways in which conflict might play out in the 21st century, and in *The Clash of Civilizations* he suggested that a new kind of conflict, one centred on cultural identity, would become the new focus of international relations. Huntington's theories, greeted with scepticism when his book first appeared in the 1990s, acquired new resonance after 9/11. *The Clash of Civilizations* is now one of the most widely-set and read works of political theory in US universities; Huntington's theories have also had a measurable impact on American policy.

In large part, this is a product of the author's problem-solving skills. *Clash* is a monument to its author's ability to generate and evaluate alternative possibilities and to make sound decisions between them – aided by an unusual talent for questioning and understanding the meaning of the evidence he was investigating. Huntington's view, that international politics after the Cold War would be neither peaceful, nor liberal, nor cooperative, ran counter to the predictions of almost all of his peers, yet his position – the product of an unusual ability to redefine an issue so as to see it in new ways – has been largely vindicated by events ever since.

ABOUT THE AUTHOR OF THE ORIGINAL WORK

American political scientist **Samuel P. Huntington** was born in 1927 in New York City, and began studying Yale University when he was just 16. He spent most of his career as a professor at Harvard University, but also helped launch the magazine *Foreign Policy* and served as a member of the United States' National Security Council in the 1970s. Huntington's work had a huge impact on US foreign policy debates after the 9/11 terrorist attacks on America in 2001, and it still fuels the current debate around the West's relationship with Islam. Huntington died in 2008, aged 81.

ABOUT THE AUTHOR OF THE ANALYSIS

Riley Quinn holds master's degrees in politics and international relations from both LSE and the University of Oxford.

ABOUT MACAT

GREAT WORKS FOR CRITICAL THINKING

Macat is focused on making the ideas of the world's great thinkers accessible and comprehensible to everybody, everywhere, in ways that promote the development of enhanced critical thinking skills.

It works with leading academics from the world's top universities to produce new analyses that focus on the ideas and the impact of the most influential works ever written across a wide variety of academic disciplines. Each of the works that sit at the heart of its growing library is an enduring example of great thinking. But by setting them in context – and looking at the influences that shaped their authors, as well as the responses they provoked – Macat encourages readers to look at these classics and game-changers with fresh eyes. Readers learn to think, engage and challenge their ideas, rather than simply accepting them.

'Macat offers an amazing first-of-its-kind tool for interdisciplinary learning and research. Its focus on works that transformed their disciplines and its rigorous approach, drawing on the world's leading experts and educational institutions, opens up a world-class education to anyone.'

Andreas Schleicher
Director for Education and Skills, Organisation for Economic Co-operation and Development

'Macat is taking on some of the major challenges in university education … They have drawn together a strong team of active academics who are producing teaching materials that are novel in the breadth of their approach.'

Prof Lord Broers,
former Vice-Chancellor of the University of Cambridge

'The Macat vision is exceptionally exciting. It focuses upon new modes of learning which analyse and explain seminal texts which have profoundly influenced world thinking and so social and economic development. It promotes the kind of critical thinking which is essential for any society and economy. This is the learning of the future.'

Rt Hon Charles Clarke, former UK Secretary of State for Education

'The Macat analyses provide immediate access to the critical conversation surrounding the books that have shaped their respective discipline, which will make them an invaluable resource to all of those, students and teachers, working in the field.'

Professor William Tronzo, University of California at San Diego

WAYS IN TO THE TEXT

KEY POINTS

- Samuel Huntington (1927–2008) was an influential American political theorist based at Harvard University in the United States.

- He argued that international relations after the Cold War* would be dictated by conflict between cultures, not between ideologies.

- *Clash* helped to redefine US foreign policy after 9/11* and it still fuels the debate around the West's relationship with Islam.

Who Was Samuel Huntington?

Samuel Huntington is widely considered to be one of the greatest political scientists of the late twentieth century. He studied and taught at some of the most prestigious universities in the United States and many regard him as the definitive American thinker on the links between cultural identity, economic development, and national security.

He was born in 1927 in New York City and by the age of 16 was a student at Yale University. He earned his first degree at 18, and at 23 he had a PhD from Harvard University, along with a teaching position. He taught there for more than half a century and during that time was called upon as an advisor to a series of leaders and policymakers. He died on Christmas Eve, 2008, aged 81.

Huntington wrote influential books that tackled some of the biggest political issues of the day. *Political Order in Changing Societies*[1] looked at the ways in which political systems work. *The Third Wave: Democratization in the Late Twentieth Century*[2] attempted to explain why more than 60 countries adopted democracy between 1974 and 2000, and *The Clash of Civilizations and the Remaking of World Order* laid down his theories on world politics after the end of the Cold War.

Huntington spent most of his career at Harvard, where he was both Albert J. Weatherhead University Professor of Political Science and President of the John M. Olin Institute for Strategic Studies. He helped found *Foreign Policy*, a magazine about international politics. Huntington is most famous for being an academic, but he also lent his expertise to the American government. In 1977 and 1978, during President Jimmy Carter's* administration, he served on the National Security Council.

What Does *The Clash of Civilizations* Say?

Huntington believed that conflict in the twenty-first century would be very different from conflict in the twentieth century. Instead of opposing ideologies causing tension around the world, he argued that problems would arise from a "clash" of competing cultures.

In *The Clash of Civilizations and the Remaking of World Order*, Huntington predicted that world power would be redistributed on the basis of civilizations that share cultural values and practices. Conflict would arise along what he called the "fault lines" between cultures, over deep-seated differences in areas such as religious beliefs and how people are governed.

Huntington saw the end of the Cold War between the United States and the Soviet Union* as a watershed moment for world politics. The political, military, and economic stand-off between these two superpowers would make way for a new kind of conflict as cultural identity became more important in politics. Huntington said that shared religion, history, heritage, and language would bring some states together in the form of a civilization in which everyone shared common goals. He believed that cultural similarities would drive the actions of such civilizations, with cultural differences creating the war zones between different civilizations and sometimes between members of the same civilization.

For decades following World War II,* the battle between different political ideas—such as capitalism* versus communism*—was at the heart of much global conflict. Huntington, however, believed that people fighting over differences in culture, not differences in ideology, was the usual state of affairs throughout history and that the end of the Cold War spelled a return to the norm.

Huntington argued that international politics after the Cold War would be neither peaceful nor liberal nor cooperative. Instead, relations would be characterized by several civilizations jockeying for position and influence along cultural lines. These civilizations included:

- a Western civilization,* encompassing Europe, North America, and Oceania
- a Sinic civilization,* encompassing China and its "near abroad" (including Korea and Vietnam)
- an Islamic civilization,* stretching from Morocco to Indonesia
- an Orthodox civilization,* including Russia and much of Eastern Europe.

Huntington wrote that these civilizations were set to become the main centers of power in the new world order. "Cultural communities," he argued, "are replacing Cold War blocs, and the fault lines between civilizations are becoming the central lines of conflict in global politics."[3]

Huntington was concerned with America's position and influence in the post-Cold War era and in particular with its decline in relation to other states. In *The Clash of Civilizations* he set out his view of how civilizations across the world relate to each other. Huntington went on to argue that the West's problem with Islam "is not Islamic fundamentalism. It is Islam [itself]."[4] According to him, Western and Islamic civilizations are both so arrogant and so intolerant that they are unable to coexist peacefully on the same planet. American neoconservatives—members of a political movement that promotes free markets and individual liberty—used Huntington's theory of a "clash" between Western and Islamic cultures to justify the controversial "War on Terror."* The War on Terror was the term commonly used to describe American-led actions throughout the Middle East against non-state "terrorist" groups, including al-Qaeda. Meanwhile, far-right groups around the world have used it to justify Islamophobia*—dislike of or prejudice against Islam.

Why Does *The Clash of Civilizations* Matter?

Studying *Clash* helps to build an understanding of what the Cold War meant for global politics. It is useful in understanding how trends in global politics have the power to influence everyday events, and it throws light on recent American history. Understanding Huntington's text, and the responses to it, can shed light on the changing ways in which America saw its place in the world. In the 1990s, America viewed itself as the leader of a growing liberal* consensus, but after 9/11 it found itself involved in another global war. *Clash* helps readers understand the relationship between the academic world and politics, and how they can define each other's concerns and questions.

Clash is an excellent introduction to critical thinking because its underlying assumptions about different cultures are easy to identify and it presents an elegant, forceful, and persuasive argument. However, Huntington has been criticized for making sweeping judgments without any evidence to back them up, and the book's problems in this regard are significant. In other words, while his argument is coherent, his reliance on assumptions about cultures, without any supporting evidence, is a problem. This has led certain thinkers to argue that *Clash* is little more than racism dressed up in the language of international relations theory. Nevertheless, students who take the time to dismantle and weigh up the arguments in *Clash* will be better equipped to do the same to texts whose assumptions and problems are less obvious.

The lasting importance of *Clash* lies in its impact on US politics and policy. Specifically, the book coincided with the rise of anti-Muslim sentiment in the West. Huntington sought to distance himself from this Islamophobia. "Neither Islam nor the West is homogeneous at all," he stated in an interview, continuing, "I don't think that it is at all useful to think in terms of two solid blocs."[5] Despite this and his opposition to the 2003 Iraq War,* Huntington is today generally associated with neoconservatism. This movement emerged in the 1960s in response to communism, but after the conclusion of the Cold War and 9/11, it switched its focus to the "War on Terror." Today, neoconservatives typically see Islam as the enemy of the West.

NOTES

1   Samuel Huntington, *Political Order in Changing Societies* (New Haven: Yale University Press, 1969).

2   Samuel Huntington, *The Third Wave: Democratization in the Late Twentieth Century* (Norman: University of Oklahoma Press, 1991).

3   Samuel Huntington, *The Clash of Civilizations and the Remaking of World Order* (London: Simon and Schuster, 2002), 126.

4   Huntington, *Clash*, 217.

5   Amina Chaudary, "The Clash of Civilizations Revisited," *Islamica Magazine*, http://www.digitalnpq.org/archive/2007_winter/14_huntington.html,

SECTION 1
INFLUENCES

MODULE 1
THE AUTHOR AND THE HISTORICAL CONTEXT

KEY POINTS

- *The Clash of Civilizations* is important to both academic and political debates about the West's position in the emerging new world order.

- Samuel Huntington was always a deeply American scholar, interested in global problems that related to American foreign policy.

- The United States believed it had just won the Cold War,* and it was in danger of becoming overconfident in its dealings with the rest of the world.

Why Read This Text?

Samuel Huntington presented a major and radical new argument in *The Clash of Civilizations.* He was convinced that future wars and political rows would run along cultural lines, rather than along the ideological ones we were used to before the end of the Cold War. Dividing lines would now depend on emotional loyalties and obligations between states and non-state actors. Groups of states that shared similar cultures, he argued, came together to form civilizations, and these would cross swords in the unfolding battle for power and influence.

Clash is one of the defining texts of a school of thought in international relations called realism.* This takes as "reality" the idea that conflict defines global politics. Huntington's theory helped renew interest in "classical" realism,* a personal, philosophical approach to understanding conflict. *Clash* also helped define the foreign policy agenda of American conservatism* and neoconservatism.*

❝ [Huntington] was anchored in American life and his American identity, but he ended up addressing so many broad questions. His degree of openness to new topics and following questions where they take him is not as often found today as when he was making his way. ❞

Professor Timothy Colton (one of Huntington's PhD students in the 1970s), Harvard University

Finally, *Clash* sounded a warning against treating the end of the Cold War as a victory for America. Huntington doubted that claiming a global triumph would spread Western ideals around the world, let alone end conflict forever. His doubts were, in many ways, confirmed by 9/11* and the subsequent "War on Terror,"* but, perversely, his theory became central to the logic of American foreign policy during this time. Some critics have suggested that by sharpening the divisions between cultures, *Clash* itself became problematic. Because Huntington cautioned Western policymakers that Islam was violent, all violence by Muslims appears to "prove" this point. Critics have argued that this position can spread ignorance and lead to damaging policy.

Author's Life

Samuel Huntington was born in New York City in 1927. At just 16 he went to Yale University, graduating two years later. He then joined the army and served in World War II*1 before returning to academia and earning his master's degree from the University of Chicago and then his PhD from Harvard University, where he began teaching at the age of 23. Huntington became a high-profile Harvard professor, dying on Martha's Vineyard, an island off the coast of Massachusetts, at the age of 81.

Huntington's work focused on American politics. One friend from Harvard remarked: "He used the American political experience as a pivot point … but soon deeply studied a globe-spanning range of topics."[2] Huntington wrote *Clash* while working at the John M. Olin Institute for Strategic Studies at Harvard, where he was director from 1989 to 1999.[3] Here he was deeply influenced by the broad strategic concerns of post-Cold War America. One key question was how America, as the most powerful state in Western civilization, should pursue its relationships with other countries. Of prime interest in this respect were Asia and the Middle East, which were experiencing a rapid rise in economic power and demographic potential at this time. Huntington's familiarity with American concerns also stems from his work in politics. He served on President Jimmy Carter's* National Security Council, and was a long-standing member of the Presidential Commission on Long-Term Integrated Strategy.

Author's Background

Huntington believed America was in danger of becoming overconfident in its newfound dominance of global politics, and overreaching itself as a result of this. This risk increased as America grappled with a number of conflicts involving other civilizations. In terms of Islamic civilization, this was the Gulf War,* whereas the Yugoslav Wars,* in which the US was also involved, were on the cusp of Western*, Orthodox* (Russian), and Islamic* civilizations.

Clash expressed a pro-establishment set of ideas as Huntington sought to protect and define American interests abroad. His cultural environment was therefore significant to the core concern of his book. *Clash* is not a detached piece of theory, but a political argument for the importance of American interests. Huntington wrote: "So long as the Muslim demographic and Asian economic surges continue … the conflicts between the West and the challenger civilizations will be more central to global politics than other lines of cleavage."[4] Huntington's writing is a warning to America and the West that it must be aware of its decline in comparison with other powers.

Worries in the United States about the growth of Islam generally during the 1990s gave rise to the book's most controversial content. Another influential thinker at the time was Bernard Lewis,* who wrote an article called "The Roots of Muslim Rage" for *The Atlantic* magazine in 1990. Lewis wrote, "For a long time now there has been a rising tide of rebellion against ... Western paramountcy, and a desire to reassert Muslim values against heretic civilizations."[5] Lewis believed there was something intrinsic to Islam that caused "an explosive mixture of rage and hatred which impels even the government of an ancient and civilized country . . . to espouse [violence]."[6] Huntington also suggests in *Clash* that of all the world's civilizations, Islam is the most predisposed to violence, saying, "Islam's borders are bloody."[7]

NOTES

1 Godfrey Hodgson, "Obituary: Samuel Huntington," *The Guardian*, http://www.theguardian.com/world/2009/jan/01/obituary-samuel-huntington, accessed January 29, 2014.

2 Corydon Ireland, "Obituaries: Samuel Huntington, 81, Political Scientist, Scholar," *Harvard Gazette*, http://news.harvard.edu/gazette/story/2009/02/samuel-huntington-81-political-scientist-scholar/, accessed January 29, 2014.

3 Ireland, "Obituaries."

4 Samuel Huntington, *The Clash of Civilizations and the Remaking of World Order* (London: Simon and Schuster, 2002), 238.

5 Bernard Lewis, "The Roots of Muslim Rage," *The Atlantic* 226, no. 3 (1990): 47.

6 Lewis, "Roots," 59.

7 Huntington, *Clash,* 217.

MODULE 2
ACADEMIC CONTEXT

KEY POINTS

- The discipline of international relations involves the quest to understand and predict how countries behave towards one another.
- Realism* is the belief that states will be in conflict and will prefer to maximize gains relative to one another, while liberalism* is a belief in states cooperating and preferring to maximize overall gains. These schools of thought argued against each other for almost a century.
- Huntington had sympathy with the more pessimistic outlook of realism.

The Work in its Context

Samuel Huntington wrote *The Clash of Civilizations* at a time when two theoretical traditions dominated political science: realism and liberalism. The debate between realism and liberalism in international relations is almost as old as the discipline itself.

Classical realism* was made popular by thinkers such as Hans Morgenthau.* In his book *Politics Among Nations*, Morgenthau wrote that "[all] politics . . . is governed by objective laws which have their roots in human nature."[1] Those laws are to do with the flawed, selfish, and proud nature of humankind. Realists were sure that conflict, not consensus, was the driving force in world politics. Liberalism was originally championed by the likes of former US president Woodrow Wilson.* His League of Nations* was founded in 1920 on the principle that states will cooperate with each other for their mutual benefit.

" Even policymakers who are contemptuous of
'theory' must rely on their own (often unstated) ideas
about how the world works in order to decide what
to do. It is hard to make good policy if one's basic
organizing principles are flawed, just as it is hard to
construct good theories without knowing a lot about
the real world. Everyone uses theories—whether he or
she knows it or not—and disagreements about policy
usually rest on more fundamental disagreements about
the basic forces that shape international outcomes. "

Stephen M. Walt, "International Relations: One World, Many Theories,"
in *Foreign Policy*

The academic discipline of international relations has always
sought to have an impact on policy. *Clash*, therefore, was an attempt
to understand and predict how states behave. Huntington never
meant the book to be an exercise in pure social science, and says
in the preface that "it aspires to present a framework, a paradigm,*
for viewing global politics that will be meaningful to scholars and
useful to policymakers."[2]

Overview of the Field

The most famous realist of the late twentieth century was Kenneth
Waltz,* whose own brand of realism was called neorealism.*
Neorealism is a purely behavioralist* theory of world politics—
meaning that it emphasized an objective, scientific approach to
explain political behavior. Neorealists believe that to survive the
anarchy*—that is, the leaderless world—of international relations,
all states act to preserve their own national interests. They do this
by assessing other states' external military capabilities and deciding
whether these capabilities either threaten their own survival

or ensure it. They then create foreign policies based on those calculations in an attempt to remain more powerful than neighboring states. According to the neorealist view, nothing else—including issues of shared culture and identity—matters. Neorealism rejects Morgenthau's focus on the failings and weaknesses of individuals, and instead assumes that state action is solely driven by calculation. According to Waltz, only "the [anarchical] structure of the system and its interacting units" explains state action.[3] Put simply, states will always prefer gains relative to other states. To them, it is more important that neighbors are worse off and less able to threaten them, than that they are better off themselves.

Neoliberalism* emerged as the main opposition to neorealism in the late twentieth century. Neoliberal thinkers such as Robert Keohane* and Joseph Nye* argued that the assumption that states are rational does "not necessarily [mean] that discord will prevail in relations among independent actors in a situation of anarchy."[4] They argued that people could observe and learn about one another, and eventually come to trust each other. This neoliberal approach assumes that nations can cooperate and overcome their fear of one another, accepting lower short-term gains relative to their neighbors, as long as they are better off in the long run.

Academic Influences

Huntington launched his landmark theory within a field characterized by debate between liberals and realists. Both of these academic traditions fielded respected thinkers with very different explanations for how the world works, and Huntington was in the realist camp. The liberal thinker whose ideas were most often held up in opposition to *Clash* was Francis Fukuyama.* Fukuyama believed that the end of the Cold War made universal acceptance of Western liberalism inevitable and that there was no need for any further development.

Huntington first set out the thinking that lay behind his book *The Clash of Civilizations* in a 1993 article entitled "The Clash of Civilizations?" for the journal *Foreign Affairs.* Huntington left off the question mark when it came to his book title—for him, the answer was "Yes." *Foreign Affairs* is dedicated to combining the concerns of academics and practitioners in the field of international relations, and it remains widely read by both. The debate between realist and liberal thinkers, however, took place primarily in the pages of even more academically oriented journals. In general, most of the realists' work appeared in *International Security*, published out of the Massachusetts Institute of Technology. Liberals, on the other hand, published most of their work in *International Organization*, a Cambridge University Press publication.

NOTES

1   Hans Morgenthau, *Politics Among Nations* (New York: McGraw Hill, 1979), 4.

2   Samuel Huntington, *The Clash of Civilizations and the Remaking of World Order* (London: Simon and Schuster, 2002), 13.

3   Kenneth Waltz, *Theory of International Politics* (Reading: Addison Wesley, 1979), 99.

4   Robert Keohane and Joseph Nye, *After Hegemony: Cooperation and Discord in the World Political Economy* (Princeton: Princeton University Press, 1984), 83.

MODULE 3
THE PROBLEM

KEY POINTS

- Academics at the time the book was first published were asking what would define world politics now that the Cold War* was over?

- Liberal universalism* holds that the West will triumph over many smaller powers, while neorealism* insists that the West is still threatened by a less stable system.

- Huntington rejected liberal universalism as arrogant and neorealism as too simplistic.

Core Question

The principal question most American international relations theorists were asking themselves in the 1990s was: now that America has won the Cold War, what should it do with its power? Samuel Huntington's answer came in *The Clash of Civilizations*. From the late 1940s to the end of the 1980s, America had a clearly defined adversary—namely, the Soviet Union* and its allies. The competing ideologies of international communism* and capitalism* meant that states could be separated into two powerful blocs: international communism on the one hand, and "the Free World"* on the other, with the rest "non-aligned."* In other words, the world system was bipolar, with power concentrated in two states.

In the wake of the Cold War, global politics underwent major reorganization into a multipolar system where there were many rising powers. "The hiatus between the Cold War and 9/11,"* wrote Richard Betts,* was a time when "conventional wisdom begged to be reinvented . . . After a worldwide contest of superpowers, the

> ❝ The triumph of the West, of the Western idea, is evident first of all in the total exhaustion of viable systematic alternatives to Western liberalism. In the past decade, there have been unmistakable changes in the intellectual climate of the world's two largest communist countries and the beginnings of significant reform movements in both. But this phenomenon extends beyond high politics, and it can be seen also in the ineluctable spread of consumerist Western culture in such diverse contexts as the peasants' markets and color television sets now omnipresent throughout China, the cooperative restaurants and clothing stores opened in the past year in Moscow, the Beethoven piped into Japanese department stores, and the rock music enjoyed alike in Prague, Rangoon, and Tehran. ❞
>
> Francis Fukuyama, "The End of History?" in *The National Interest*

only conflicts were local, numerous but minor. What would the driving force of world politics be after the twentieth century?"[1] Huntington's focus as he addressed this question was not only on predicting conflict, but also on predicting conflict from an American point of view. That included a warning to America not to overuse the power gained from its seeming global triumph.

The Participants

Two competing sets of answers to the big question—namely, what should America do with its post-Cold War power?—emerged straight after the Cold War. One set consisted of neorealist answers,* as championed by John Mearsheimer,* and the other comprised those of liberal universalism,* as argued by Francis Fukuyama.*

Neoclassical realism,* a school broadly covering Samuel Huntington's position, served as a response to both.

Fukuyama's most famous book was *The End of History and the Last Man*. In his 1989 article of the same name, Fukuyama said that "the triumph of the West, of the Western idea, is evident first of all in the total exhaustion of viable systematic alternatives to Western liberalism."[2] For him, the end of the Cold War meant that Western liberalism had become the inevitable dominant political system globally and that there was no need for any further development. This meant that history—defined as the tumult, evolution, and conflict that moves human society forward—had come to its end point.[3] Fukuyama dismissed the possibility of enduring divisions along religious or national lines mainly because religious doctrine (that of a religious Muslim state, for example) would have no appeal for anyone outside it (non-Muslims in this case).[4] Liberalism, according to Fukuyama, had emerged as the only school of thought that appeals to universal human values of recognition of everyone as equal and worthy of respect, as well as of freedom and the desire to flourish.

In stark contrast, the neorealist John Mearsheimer argued that nothing at all had changed after the Cold War. The world, he said, would continue to be defined by power play based on the relative strength of states-as-billiard-balls* (they are all roughly the same and act only in relation to outside forces). Mearsheimer's model predicted, for example, that Russia and Ukraine would see one another as rivals, rather than as natural allies, because of their long borders and large militaries.[5]

The Contemporary Debate

Huntington thought it would be very dangerous for the West to accept Fukuyama's version of the new world order, and he wrote *Clash* to debunk liberal universalism. He feared it would blind statesmen to the emerging realities of a decline in the power of America (and Western civilization* overall) relative to its competitors (especially Chinese and Islamic* civilizations). He said the end of the ideological tension between the "Free World" and communism had not made conflict obsolete, it had simply made way for a different kind of clash—one based on cultural differences. "In the emerging [post-Cold War] world," Huntington wrote, "Western belief in the universality of Western culture suffers three problems: it is false; it is immoral; and it is dangerous."[6] He said that the assumption was that "the collapse of Soviet communism meant the end of history and the universal victory of [Western] liberal democracy." However, he pointed out that "Muslims, Chinese, Indians, and others" have alternative forms of government they believe to be as legitimate as liberal democracy, or more so, and that they are likely to view the promotion of Western forms of government as aggressive.[7]

Huntington also used *Clash* to dismiss Mearsheimer's neorealist arguments, but devoted significantly less time to this criticism. He saw Mearsheimer's prediction that Russia and Ukraine would go to war as ridiculous because of the "close culture, personal, and historical links between Russia and Ukraine … [which] Mearsheimer totally ignores."[8] Huntington believed that the break-up of Ukraine along civilizational lines (it being half Western Christian and half Slavic Orthodox) would be more likely than a conflict between Russia and Ukraine based on nothing more than mutual fear of one another's capabilities.[9] This is not to say that Huntington believed Russia and Ukraine would be friendly; rather, he thought that the conflict would be more along the lines of a split Ukraine (part of it siding with Russia, part with Europe) than taking the form of a unified Ukraine pitted against Russia.

NOTES

1   Richard Betts, "Conflict or Cooperation?" *Foreign Affairs* 89, no. 6 (2010): 186.

2   Francis Fukuyama, "The End of History?" *The National Interest*, Summer (1989): 5.

3   Fukuyama, "The End of History?" 5.

4   Fukuyama, "The End of History?" 18.

5   John Mearsheimer, "The Case for a Nuclear Deterrent," *Foreign Affairs* 72 (1993): 54.

6   Samuel Huntington, *The Clash of Civilizations and the Remaking of World Order* (London: Simon and Schuster, 2002), 310.

7   Huntington, *Clash,* 66.

8   Huntington, *Clash*, 37.

9   Huntington, *Clash*, 37.

MODULE 4
THE AUTHOR'S CONTRIBUTION

KEY POINTS

- Cultural divisions between groups of states will drive future conflict, thereby defining the new world order.

- *The Clash of Civilizations* was the first "grand" theory specifically concerned with describing the post-Cold War world.

- It was deeply inspired by the pessimistic but humanistic* approach of classical realism,* especially the works of Reinhold Niebuhr.*

Author's Aims

In *The Clash of Civilizations*, Samuel Huntington put forward an ambitious new theory of how political and economic power would shift among nations in the post–Cold War era. He said that everything had changed and a different kind of conflict would remake the world order. *Clash* was designed to convince Western leaders that international tensions would increasingly spring from the clash of cultures, not from ideological rivalries as in the past. By focusing on the importance of emotional ties, *Clash* was very different from the behavioralist* theories that had been popular in the 1980s. Huntington believed that cultural divisions made Francis Fukuyama's* idea of a universal civilization impossible, and John Mearsheimer's* states–as–billiard–balls* impractical. He argued that "cultural communities," which he defined as civilizations on a global scale, "are replacing Cold War* blocs, and the fault lines between civilizations are becoming the central lines of conflict in global politics."[1]

66 The post–Cold War* world is a world of seven or eight major civilizations. Cultural commonalities and differences shape the interests, antagonisms, and associations of states. The most important countries in the world come overwhelmingly from different civilizations. The local conflicts most likely to escalate into broader wars are those between groups and states from different civilizations . . . Power is shifting from the long-predominant West to non-Western civilizations. Global politics has become multipolar and multicivilizational. 99

Samuel Huntington, *The Clash of Civilizations and the Remaking of World Order*

Huntington unveiled his ideas in his 1993 article, "*The Clash of Civilizations?*"[2] which he wrote to "set forth descriptive hypotheses as to what the future may be like." Those hypotheses center on the proposition that "differences between civilizations are real and important; civilization-consciousness is increasing; [and] conflict between civilizations will supplant ideological and other forms of conflict as the dominant global form of conflict."[3] The article set the groundwork for his theories; the seminal book, whose title omitted the question mark of the article's title, followed three years later and developed the actual theory.

Approach

Part of the importance of *Clash* stems from Huntington's ambition to produce a grand theory for the post-Cold War era. He made his case by drawing on centuries of historical evidence from every world civilization because he wanted to create a theory that was as relevant to Australia as it was to Cuba or Japan. This approach, which relies on broad generalizations, is also rooted in Huntington's belief in parsimony—the principle that things usually behave in the simplest or most economical way. He compared understanding global politics to reading a map. Someone looking to drive from one city to another needs only to know the location of the main highways, not where all the back roads are.[4] The groups that he discussed were so large that it would have been impossible for every element of his theory to apply to each culture, state, or individual while still remaining useful. "We need a map," Huntington argued, "that both portrays reality and simplifies reality."[5]

In this way, Huntington owed the prominent realist thinker Kenneth Waltz* an intellectual debt. Waltz shared Huntington's pessimism about global politics, as both thinkers assumed that they were defined by conflict rather than cooperation. He also agreed with Huntington's focus on parsimony, disagreeing merely on which variables, and how many of them, were to be taken into account. Whereas Waltz examined only the balance of power, Huntington took shared identity and cultural difference into consideration as well. Both Huntington and Waltz predicted that conflict was inevitable in global politics, and both believed in relatively simple, "highway map"-style theories.

Contribution in Context

Huntington saw his original contribution as recycling an older style of classical realist* thinking. He claimed in an interview to be a "child of" American theologian and classical realist Reinhold Niebuhr,* owing a specific debt to his "compelling combination of morality and practical realism."[6] In his 1952 book *The Irony of American History*, Niebuhr predicted that if it were victorious against the Soviets, a triumphant America would attempt to carry its victory around the world and to use its power recklessly.[7] He noted, famously, that the rest of the world was "now exercised about the possibilities of misuse of our power.

We would do well to understand the legitimacy of such fears rather than resent their seeming injustice."[8] Huntington echoed Niebuhr's concern when he wrote that "the principal responsibility of Western leaders . . . is not to attempt to reshape other civilizations in the image of the West, which is beyond their declining power, but to preserve, protect and renew the unique qualities of Western civilization."[9] This is one of the reasons *Clash* is often thought of as one of the first works in neoclassical realism.* It was among the first major works to bring the concerns of classical realism into a post–Cold War era.

NOTES

1   Samuel Huntington, *The Clash of Civilizations and the Remaking of World Order* (London: Simon and Schuster, 2002), 126.

2   Samuel Huntington, "The Clash of Civilizations?" *Foreign Affairs* 72, no. 3 (1993): 24.

3   Huntington, "The Clash of Civilizations?" 48.

4   Huntington, *Clash*, 31.

5   Huntington, *Clash*, 31.

6   Robert Kaplan, "Looking the World in the Eye," *The Atlantic*, http://www.theatlantic.com/magazine/archive/2001/12/looking-the-world-in-the-eye/302354/, accessed January 29, 2014.

7   Reinhold Niebuhr, *The Irony of American History* (London: Nisbet & Co, 1952), 113–14.

8   Niebuhr, *The Irony of American History*, 113–14.

9   Huntington, *Clash*, 311.

SECTION 2
IDEAS

MODULE 5
MAIN IDEAS

KEY POINTS

- In the post-Cold War* world, cultural rather than ideological differences between civilizations will cause conflict between states.

- Cultural ties underpin political decision-making as the distribution of power in the world shifts from America versus Russia to different bases around the world.

- Huntington's theory is presented simply and directly as a unified idea for an American readership—namely, change the distribution of power, and you change the rules of the game.

Key Themes

Samuel Huntington's argument in *The Clash of Civilizations* was that with the end of the Cold War, it is now culture that governs political action, and that the world system of civilizations grouped together by shared cultures determines who is an ally and who is an enemy.

Huntington's whole argument in *Clash* rests on his core assumption that global politics were fundamentally changed by the end of the Cold War. "The end of the Cold War," he wrote, "has not ended conflict but has rather given rise to new identities rooted in culture and to new patterns of conflict among groups from different cultures, which at the broadest level are civilizations."[1]

Huntington had a very particular sense of what he meant by the term "civilization." "What do we mean when we talk of civilization?" he asked in his 1993 article "The Clash of Civilizations?" in which he first set out his theory. "A civilization," he went on, "is a cultural

> **❝** The underlying problem for the West is not Islamic fundamentalism.* It is Islam, a different civilization whose people are convinced of the superiority of their culture and are obsessed with the inferiority of their power. The problem for Islam* is not the CIA [Central Intelligence Agency]* or the US Department of Defense. It is the West, a different civilization whose people are convinced of the universality of their culture, and believe that their superior, if declining, power imposes on them the obligation to extend that culture throughout the world. **❞**
>
> Samuel Huntington, *The Clash of Civilizations and the Remaking of World Order*

entity. Villages, regions, ethnic groups, nationalities, religious groups, all have distinct cultures at different levels of cultural heterogeneity* … A civilization is thus the highest cultural grouping of people and the broadest level of cultural identity people have."[2] These cultural groupings are not "actors," as states are. Civilizations are made up of many different actors with a shared outlook. They see one another as similar and those outside the civilization as different. So neighboring civilizations would naturally come into conflict, according to Huntington. He believed countries from different civilizations would struggle for relative power over one another, and "competitively promote their particular political and religious values."[3]

Exploring the Ideas

Huntington sums up his main theme in the following statement: "Cultural commonalities and differences shape the interests, antagonisms, and associations of states."[4] He did not believe that civilizations were the players in world politics. That position, he thought, was still usually occupied by states. Cultural difference and similarity between groups of states (civilizations) would determine the ways in which countries relate to one another, and factors such as shared religion, history, heritage, and language would tie a group of states together into a civilization.[5]

As an example, Huntington offers the splintering of Yugoslavia, a state bordering three civilizations (Western,* Orthodox,* and Islamic*). During the Cold War it was held together by the ideology of communism,* but afterwards it experienced an ethnic civil war (the Yugoslav Wars).* "In the former Yugoslavia," Huntington wrote, "Russia backs Orthodox Serbia, Germany promotes Catholic Croatia, Muslim* countries rally to the support of the Bosnian government" not because of some abstract notion of "the national interest," but because "people rally to those with similar ancestry, religion, language, values, and institutions."[6]

According to philosopher Imre Lakatos's* definition of a social scientific theory, it is the way in which Huntington treats culture as the driving factor in international decision-making that forms the "hard core" of his paradigm.* Huntington also made a number of other assumptions in order to predict how world politics would develop. Most important among these was the assumption of a Western decline compared with other civilizations, especially the Islamic and Chinese. Having chosen civilizations as his unit of analysis, Huntington went on to propose how these units would behave toward each other in the future. "The most dangerous clashes of the future," he wrote, "are likely to arise from Western arrogance, Islamic intolerance, and Sinic* assertiveness."[7]

The second main theme running through Huntington's work is the significance of polarity*—that is, the distribution of power within the international system—in determining what happens. Huntington borrows his definition of an international system from the famous international relations theorist Hedley Bull:* "Two or more states [which] have sufficient contact between them, and have sufficient impact on one another's decisions, to cause them to behave . . . as parts of a whole."[8] The Cold War world was bipolar, meaning there were two major power centers—the United States and the Soviet Union*—around which world politics tended to focus. For most of the time each had nuclear weapons pointed at the other in a balancing act of mutually assured destruction.* In this world, only one division (what Huntington terms "cleavage*") mattered. But in a post-Cold War world, Huntington wrote, "No single cleavage dominates, and multiple cleavages exist between the West and other civilizations and among the many non-Wests."[9]

To explain this, he points to the history of the atom bomb. "The role of nuclear weapons . . . in the post-Cold War world is . . . the opposite of that during the Cold War" because there is no mutually assured destruction.[10] Instead, the United States, with its strong nuclear and conventional arsenal, makes all those who identify as its competitors (especially Orthodox, Sinic, and Islamic civilizations) feel the need to pursue nuclear weapons programs themselves. At the same time, the United States is trying to stop them. The post-Cold War arms race is not, Huntington argues, "a case of build up versus build up," as it was during the Cold War. Instead, it is "a case of build up versus hold down."[11] The world system, in other words, is of such importance within Huntington's theory that something that has one meaning in one world system can mean exactly the opposite as soon as the balance of power shifts.

Language and Expression
Huntington's framework of ideas explains why he was so adamant that the United States should not behave arrogantly in the aftermath of the Cold War. His focus on the distribution of power in the international system showed the reader that victory in the Cold War did not

translate into victory after the Cold War—it translated into an entirely new game. The players of that new game, Huntington suggested, were civilizations. In essence, his framework of ideas defined the rules of the game and the nature of the players and enabled Huntington to make his predictions.

NOTES

1   Samuel Huntington, *The Clash of Civilizations and the Remaking of World Order* (London: Simon and Schuster, 2002), 130.

2   Samuel Huntington, "The Clash of Civilizations?" *Foreign Affairs* 72, no. 3 (1993): 24.

3   Huntington, "Clash," 29.

4   Huntington, *Clash*, 29.

5   Huntington, *Clash*, 125.

6   Huntington, *Clash*, 126–7.

7   Huntington, *Clash*, 183.

8   Hedley Bull, quoted in Huntington, *Clash,* 54.

9   Huntington, *Clash*, 54.

10 Huntington, *Clash*, 189.

11 Huntington, *Clash*, 190.

MODULE 6
SECONDARY IDEAS

KEY POINTS

- The sudden changes that modernization brings to societies destabilize developing states and encourage religious revivals.

- It's important to understand these underlying factors in order to grasp why America's power is in decline compared with other states.

- Huntington's argument that cultural factors are central to economic as well as strategic cooperation has often been ignored.

Other Ideas

Samuel Huntington's aim in *The Clash of Civilizations* was to describe the world in terms of separate civilizations and to explain how he believed they related to one another. Dividing the world up into shared cultures was the starting point for his theory about why and how countries drew up their battle lines.

Central to *Clash* was Huntington's belief that the power of the West was in decline following the end of the Cold War.* He sought to convince readers that the relative power balance between Western and non-Western (especially Chinese and Islamic*) civilizations was shifting in favor of non-Western power. Huntington was particularly interested in two reasons for this change—namely, the effects of modernization, and the growing role of religious belief.

Whereas many liberal* thinkers, such as Francis Fukuyama,* believed that modernization would inevitably bring Western-style secularism (the separation of government from religious institutions)

> 66 Becoming a modern society is about industrialization, urbanization, and rising levels of literacy, education, and wealth. The qualities that make a society Western,* in contrast, are special: the classical legacy, Christianity,* the separation of church and state, the rule of law, civil society. 99
>
> Samuel Huntington, *The Clash of Civilizations and the Remaking of World Order*

to those societies it pervaded, Huntington believed the opposite would happen. Where liberals saw development as a process that resulted in tolerant, rational, pragmatic, progressive, humanistic, and secular societies, Huntington saw modernization as a destabilizing force. He also explored the global resurgence of religion as a factor in conflict, using theorist Gilles Kepel's* French term *la revanche de dieu* (the revenge of God).

Exploring the Ideas

Huntington said the collapse of ideology that came with modernization created a vacuum that was being filled by religious revivals. These, he believed, were "anti-secular, anti-universal, and, except in their [Western] Christian manifestations, anti-Western."[1] Huntington argued, "The Islamic Resurgence is both a product of and an effort to come to grips with modernization ... [Development undermines] traditional village and clan ties and [creates] alienation as an identity crisis."[2] Far from increasing the appeal of Western culture, then, modernization increases the appeal of non-Western culture, and encourages anti-Western feeling. So not only does modernization generate religious revivals, it destabilizes global politics. Huntington claims that modernization has triggered "the growing power of non-Western societies [and] the revival of non-Western cultures throughout the world."[3]

Huntington believed that a new balance of power would define the politics that existed between civilizations, in a way that looked problematic for the West. He claimed the West's three main interests were:

- "to maintain its military superiority" through treaties that prevented the build-up of non-conventional weapons
- "to promote Western political values" by aggressively pushing democracy and human rights abroad
- "to protect the cultural, social, and ethnic integrity of Western societies" by controlling immigration from non-Western societies.[4]

Huntington argued that the West was in trouble on all three fronts. For example, the United States' policy of holding down states that were attempting to acquire nuclear weapons had failed to prevent India, Pakistan, and North Korea from having them. Successful attempts to promote democracy abroad had more often than not resulted in leaders who had risen to power on an anti-American, anti-Western platform. And finally, as the "Third World"[*] enjoyed a population boom, young people were moving to the West from non-Western societies without a like-for-like exchange, thereby diluting Western cultures without diluting non-Western cultures. All in all, Huntington concluded, "the changing balance of power among civilizations makes it more and more difficult for the West to achieve its goals."[5]

Overlooked

Huntington also considered how the "new game" of global politics would affect attempts to build economic relationships. "The roots of economic cooperation," he argued, "are in cultural commonality."[6] Put simply, trade went more smoothly when the people involved had a broadly similar way of life. When Huntington wrote *Clash*, "regionalism" (where a sense of identity grew out of people's place on the map) was a hot topic in political debate. Huntington argued that it was culture—not geography—that defined how successfully people traded with each other.

"Regionalism," therefore, was an empty concept, since "regions are geographical not political or cultural entities."[7] Huntington pointed to the failure of the East Asian Economic Caucus* in comparison with the success of the European Union* (EU) as evidence for this position. Japan, he argued, is a civilization that is distinct from China (which is, in turn, distinct from Islamic Indonesia and Malaysia), and as such it was reluctant to join the caucus. He explained that Japan was "a lone country with few cultural connections with its neighbors," and this explained its refusal to enter into a robust regional agreement.[8] Cultural similarities across the EU, on the other hand, he argued, have meant that it "has moved furthest down the integration road with a common market and many elements of an economic union."[9]

NOTES

1   Samuel Huntington, *The Clash of Civilizations and the Remaking of World Order* (London: Simon and Schuster, 2002), 100.

2   Huntington, *Clash*, 116.

3   Huntington, *Clash*, 92.

4   Huntington, *Clash*, 186.

5   Huntington, *Clash*, 206.

6   Huntington, *Clash*, 135.

7   Huntington, *Clash*, 136.

8   Huntington, *Clash*, 133.

9   Huntington, *Clash*, 131.

MODULE 7
ACHIEVEMENT

KEY POINTS

- Samuel Huntington designed a grand theory for understanding how politics will evolve across the world.

- The framework is presented exclusively in terms of Western interests and Huntington's American-centric picture of the world.

- A lack of direct research and use of broad strokes means that Huntington's picture of how the world works is based on generalization rather than fact.

Assessing the Argument

Samuel Huntington wanted to create a grand theory of international conflict that would explain the post-Cold War* world to his fellow Americans. A distinguished academic who had often been welcome at the White House, he had the interests of the United States firmly in mind when making his predictions. *The Clash of Civilizations* brought him worldwide attention and a reputation as a controversial voice in the field of international relations at the close of the twentieth century.

Clash was an ambitious attempt to explain how world politics would be rewritten along cultural lines rather than continuing to adhere to the ideological rules that had dominated before the end of the Cold War. Huntington was an intellectual heavyweight and his theory was logically coherent—he did not deviate from his argument, nor did he fail to pull it together. At the outset, he stated that his intention was to present a new theoretical framework that would help people to understand global politics writ large. He began with an

“ During the coming decades, Asian economic growth will have deeply destabilizing effects on the Western-dominated established international order . . . Meanwhile, Muslim population growth will be a destabilizing force for both Muslim societies and their neighbors . . . As a result, the early years of the twenty-first century are likely to see an ongoing resurgence of non-Western power and culture and the clash of the peoples of non-Western civilizations with the West and with each other. ”

Samuel Huntington, *The Clash of Civilizations and the Remaking of World Order*

analysis of the balance of power within the system, identifying his relevant variables and showing how they might interact. The criticism he received, though, was not so much about what he included, but rather concerned what he left out. Some felt that his evidence for the broad-brush assertions in *Clash* did not withstand scrutiny.

Achievement In Context

Huntington wrote *Clash* from a well-established position within the Western academic world. His text was widely read and discussed at the time and is still argued over today. Though he first set out his ideas in 1993 and the book was published in 1996, the events of 9/11* in 2001 brought *Clash* worldwide attention from both supporters and opponents of his theories. Huntington was not discouraged from his work, nor did he experience restrictions or censorship. As a Harvard professor, he was very securely situated in the American academic mainstream. He received financial support from numerous organizations that encouraged his research. It cannot be denied, however, that the text is Western-centric.

Huntington spent a disproportionate amount of time addressing Western concerns. His justification for this was that "the West is and will remain for years to come the most powerful civilization. Yet its power relative to that of other civilizations is declining . . . A central axis of post-Cold War world politics is thus the interaction of Western power and culture with the power and culture of non-Western civilizations."[1] Huntington was making clear to the reader his assumption that the West, especially America, comprised the most important group of states in world politics. That is why his analysis was largely written in terms of the "West and the rest."

Limitations

The research for *Clash*, by and large, was not the kind of rigorous analytical work that can actually define policy. Instead, this research was performed over a lifetime of international relations scholarship. The text is full of citations—from journals, books, and studies undertaken by Huntington's fellow academics—but this mostly performs the function of positioning *Clash* in its academic environment. Huntington himself did not engage in much research "on the ground." In the aftermath of his 1993 article that was a forerunner to his book, he went on debate tours that "exposed [him] to all the major civilizations except Hinduism,"[2] but the material that resulted from this was most often used for color rather than to help build the argument. The argument itself relied on Huntington's knowledge of world history and culture.

Huntington came in for significant criticism from postcolonial* theorists, whose work seeks to expose the legacies of imperialism.* Their damning claim was that Huntington was largely reproducing Western biases and calling it international relations theory, rather than doing real research. Edward Said* suggested that Huntington's take on Islam was a culturally biased and essentializing* viewpoint. Said argued that Huntington viewed Islam not as it is, but as it is seen by an alarmist West. Said asked: "Did [Huntington] canvass 100 Indonesians,

200 Moroccans, 500 Egyptians and 50 Bosnians?"[3] He argued that *Clash* was "a gimmick," and served only to reinforce divisions between Muslims and Westerners, especially as "the official discourse" in the early days after 9/11 "drew its vocabulary" from *Clash*.*

NOTES

1   Samuel Huntington, *The Clash of Civilizations and the Remaking of World Order* (London: Simon and Schuster, 2002), 29.

2   Huntington, Clash, 14.

3   Edward Said, "The Clash of Ignorance," *The Nation*, http://www.thenation.com/article/clash-ignorance, accessed February 1, 2014.

MODULE 8
PLACE IN THE AUTHOR'S WORK

KEY POINTS

- Huntington's body of work resists overall classification because he focused on numerous topics throughout his life.

- *Clash* even seemed to contradict the rest of his work, especially on the key topic of whether the move to democracy can work in non-Western countries.

- *Clash* is Huntington's most famous book, but his earlier works are also considered to be important texts.

Positioning

Samuel Huntington wrote *The Clash of Civilizations* in 1996, towards the end of an academic career that began in 1952. It shares a theme with all his writing—concerning the power of identity to shape history and political decision-making. His 1969 book *Political Order in Changing Societies* argued that rapid modernization in developing countries produces political instability by raising political awareness.[1] This was echoed in *Clash* (though it was not the book's main argument): "The Islamic resurgence is both a product of and an effort to come to grips with modernization . . . [T]hese developments undermine traditional village and clan ties and create alienation as an identity crisis."[2] In other words, Huntington's assumption that modernization causes political turmoil was virtually unchanged.

In 1991, Huntington published *The Third Wave: Democratization in the Late Twentieth Century*, which seems at odds with *Political Order*

> **❝** The primary thesis of this book is that [violence
> and instability in developing countries is] in large
> part the product of rapid social change and the rapid
> mobilization of new groups into politics coupled with
> the slow development of political institutions. **❞**
>
> Samuel Huntington, *Political Order in Changing Societies*

and the argument he would develop in *Clash*. In *The Third Wave*,
when considering the major limiting factors in the democratization
of a state, Huntington included the role of culture and came to a
subtly different conclusion from his later one in *Clash*. Democratic
Islam,* or democratic Confucianism,* according to Huntington in
The Third Wave, may be contradictions in terms, "but a democracy
in a Confucian [or Islamic] society may not be. The real question
is which elements in Islam and Confucianism are favorable to
democracy, and how and under what circumstances these can
supersede the undemocratic aspects of these cultural traditions."[3]
In *Clash*, Huntington had become less convinced about the
possibility of, for example, democracy developing in an Islamic
culture. He argued that Arab culture would associate modernization
with deepening Islamism, rather than with democratization.
While, he argues, modernization leads to a demand for liberal
political institutions and democracy in most countries, "Islamism*
was a functional substitute for the democratic opposition to
authoritarianism* in Christian societies, and it was in large part the
product of similar causes."[4] In other words, he believed that people
in these countries would turn to their religion rather than to the
ballot box as modernization took hold.

This seems to be a significant tension between the theories and
ideas in Huntington's various books. In *The Third Wave*, he appeared
to merge modernization, democratization, and Westernization. He

left them separate in *Political Order* and, more importantly, in *Clash*, in which he wrote that "modernization . . . does not necessarily mean Westernization."[5] In *Clash*, an Islamic state could both modernize and have a non-democratic government, whereas in Western culture (which favors democracy) this is not possible. In *The Third Wave*, on the other hand, Huntington argued that Islamic states would democratize at least partly through modernization, despite the existence of non-democratic trends in Islamic culture.

Integration

It is difficult to draw a straight line through Huntington's thought because he never committed to one idea, or even one object of analysis. The philosopher Isaiah Berlin* said there were two kinds of thinkers: hedgehogs and foxes. A hedgehog always sticks to one idea and always sees the world through the "lens" of that one idea. A fox tests out different ideas and sees the world through different "lenses."[6] According to Gideon Rose,* who was Huntington's former student and the editor of *Foreign Affairs*, Huntington was a fox.[7] He was such a classic fox that it is better to see his overall body of work as responding to the themes that were important at the time, rather than as building on one idea.

Take the seemingly contradictory positions Huntington sets out in *The Third Wave* and *Clash*. In one sense, the difference boils down to the way he worked. In *Clash* he was analyzing the broad strokes of a culture, whereas he allowed for more subtlety in *The Third Wave*. Thus, in *Clash* he decided that most of Islam was mostly incompatible with democracy and took it from there. In *The Third Wave* he identified the elements of Islam he believed to be more compatible with democracy, and reasoned from that position.

Huntington tended to deal in general themes rather than analyzing details. He wrote in his first book that "actual personalities, institutions, and beliefs do not fit into neat logical categories . . . [but] neat logical categories are necessary if man is to think profitably about the real world."[8]

The differences between his various theories boil down to what was going on in the world at the time that Huntington was writing any particular work, as he always tailored his explanations to current affairs. Huntington wrote *The Third Wave* at a time when political scientists around the world were trying to explain why so many states in Eastern Europe, Latin America, and sub-Saharan Africa appeared to adopt democracy so quickly. Huntington answered that question. By 1993, in the aftermath of the first Gulf War* and during the Yugoslav Wars,* the same political scientists were trying to explain why conflict carried on despite the end of the Cold War.* Huntington answered that question.

Significance

Huntington's overall body of work has been extremely influential, but there is debate among scholars as to which of his books is more powerful. Some say *Political Order* and others prefer *Clash*. His former student Minxin Pei* reflected, "Sam had a unique gift that might be called an 'Intellectual Midas Touch'—whatever he wrote became a classic."[9]

But that Midas touch extended to many disciplines, and one result of the enduring fame of *Clash* is that the significance of *The Third Wave* to the study of democracy has been forgotten. *The Third Wave* went on to help define the field of democratization studies. It set the groundwork for a theory now referred to as the transition paradigm.* That model defined the way both practitioners and scholars of democratization believed that transitions to democracy happened. In a sense, *Clash* helped make Huntington popular and famous, but it also obscured his equally important work in other disciplines.

NOTES

1   Samuel Huntington, *Political Order in Changing Societies* (New Haven: Yale University Press, 1969), 3.

2   Samuel Huntington, *The Clash of Civilizations and the Remaking of World Order* (London: Simon and Schuster, 2002), 116.

3   Samuel Huntington, "Democracy's Third Wave," *Journal of Democracy* 2, no. 2 (1991): 30.

4   Huntington, *Clash,* 114.

5   Huntington, *Clash*, 78.

6   Isaiah Berlin, *The Hedgehog and the Fox: An Essay on Tolstoy's View of History* (New York: Simon and Schuster, 1986), 1.

7   Gideon Rose, "Introduction," in *Foreign Affairs Presents the Clash of Civilizations? The Debate: Twentieth Anniversary Edition* (Washington: Foreign Affairs, 2013), 2.

8   Samuel Huntington, *The Soldier and the State* (Cambridge: Belknap Press, 1981), vii.

9   Minxin Pei, quoted in Katherine Yester, "Samuel Huntington, 1927–2008," *Foreign Policy*, http://www.foreignpolicy.com/articles/2009/02/16/samuel_huntington_1927_2008, accessed January 30, 2014.

SECTION 3
IMPACT

MODULE 9
THE FIRST RESPONSES

KEY POINTS

- *Clash* was criticized for exaggerating the power of cultural differences to cause wars, painting a simplistic and unrealistic portrait of complex societies, and making racist assumptions about non-Western cultures.

- Huntington denied being an Islamophobe* and said he did not argue in his book that Muslims were inherently violent.

- The book was published years before 9/11* and was easy to criticize as alarmist because new threats to America had not yet materialized.

Criticism

The most fundamental criticism of Samuel Huntington's *The Clash of Civilizations* was that it overestimated the power of culture to drive conflict. "Islam's borders are bloody," wrote Huntington, going on to say that "the fundamental problem for the West is not Islamic fundamentalism. It is Islam . . . the problem for Islam is not [any particular institution of the West]. It is the West . . . These are the basic ingredients that fuel conflict between Islam and the West."[1] Islam and the West, in other words, are essentialized*— that is, they are defined by a set of characteristics—and they are also static and monolithic.*

Fouad Ajami* responded to the 1993 "Clash of Civilizations?" article in *Foreign Affairs* (where Huntington first discussed his *Clash* theory) by saying that this "civilizational paradigm"* was too tidy and detached from reality. "Huntington," he wrote, "has found his

❝ It seems to me that unless we emphasize and maximize a spirit of cooperation and humanistic exchange, and here I don't speak simply of uninformed delight or amateurish enthusiasm for the exotic but rather a profound existential commitment and labor on behalf of the other . . . we are going to end up superficially and stridently banging the drum for our culture in opposition to all the others. **❞**

Edward Said, early postcolonial theorist, from his lecture "The Myth of the *Clash of Civilizations,*" 1998

civilizations whole and intact, watertight under an eternal sky . . . For this student of history and culture, civilizations have always been messy creatures."[2] Although Ajami agreed that states and statesmen may be shaped by cultural backgrounds, he went on to say, ". . . but let us be clear: civilizations do not control states."[3] Ajami suggested a number of instances in support of this counter-argument; for example, he argued that "the battle lines in the Caucasus . . . follow the interests of states," while in the tension between Christian Armenia and Muslim Azerbaijan, Muslim Iran "cast religious zeal and [civilizational] fidelity to the wind," and supported Armenia.[4]

The most enduring attack on Huntington's ideas, however, argues not that he underestimated state power, but that he was racist. One of the strongest charges leveled against Huntington was that he assumed that aspects of people's identities (such as their race and religion) would inevitably make them act in a certain way. He was also very strongly criticized, particularly by Edward Said* and Amartya Sen,* for his views that Islam was especially violent.

"Huntington," wrote Said after 9/11,* "is an ideologist, someone who wants to make 'civilizations' and 'identities' into what they are not: shut-down, sealed-off entities that have been purged of the myriad currents and countercurrents that animate human history."[5] But rather than bring his criticism around to reassert state power, as Ajami had, Said took a different route. He wrote that "[Huntington's strong, warmongering] rhetoric is used inappropriately," citing Huntington's basic idea of a war between Islam and the West at its root, "with scant attention to complex histories that defy such reductiveness."*[6] Said believed that Huntington's thesis in *Clash* was a self-fulfilling prophecy—that those who were encouraged by its simplistic idea that there is a war between Islam and the West created a war out of the actions of "a small group of deranged militants" on 9/11. Amartya Sen summarized the entire position against Huntington tidily: "Identity," he said, "is not destiny."[7]

Responses

Huntington answered his critics by suggesting that they had misunderstood *Clash*. He felt that his critics either didn't understand how much power he assigned to civilizations, or mistook the way in which he thought of civilizations.

He responded to critics of the 1993 *Foreign Affairs* article with another article, titled "If Not Civilizations, What?" Given that his critics had suggested that his civilizational paradigm was too narrow, the thrust of this article was to ask, "Can any other paradigm do better?"[8] In response to those (such as Ajami) who suggested that his theory appeared to minimize the role of the state in favor of the "civilization," Huntington restated his belief that civilizations define the interests of states.[9]

After the publication of *Clash*, Huntington gave an interview to *Islamica Magazine* to respond to accusations that he was an Islamophobe.* Huntington was asked, "Doesn't making a dichotomous distinction between the West and Islam imply that there is a uniformity within those two categories?" Huntington replied, "Neither Islam nor the West is homogeneous at all. I don't think that it is at all useful to think in terms of two solid blocs."[10] In direct response to Amartya Sen's argument that "[i]dentity is not destiny," he argued: "I think that statement by Amartya Sen is totally wrong . . . What I argue in my book . . . is that the basis of association and antagonism among countries has changed over time."[11] In other words, he was not claiming that Muslims were inherently violent people. He was claiming that, taken as a bloc, the "Muslim world" had been engaged in more conflict in recent memory than other parts of the world.

Conflict and Consensus

Clash was published five years before the events of 9/11, which included the attack on the World Trade Center in New York. When Huntington's 1996 book appeared it was widely read, but in general critics thought that his analysis was shallow and alarmist because no hard evidence appeared to bear it out. Huntington predicted that serious foreign policy threats to America would emerge after the Cold War*—creating the same kind of problems as those that had been posed by the Soviet Union* during the Cold War. It wasn't until 2001 that such threats actually emerged, but critics continued to believe that *Clash* remained a profound misreading of the world.

NOTES

1   Samuel Huntington, *The Clash of Civilizations and the Remaking of World Order* (London: Simon and Schuster, 2002), 217.

2   Fouad Ajami, "The Summoning," *Foreign Affairs 72*, no. 4 (1993) 4: 2.

3   Ajami, "The Summoning," 9.

4   Ajami, "The Summoning," 8.

5   Edward Said, "The Clash of Ignorance," *The Nation*, http://www.thenation.com/article/clash-ignorance, accessed February 1, 2014.

6   Said, "Clash of Ignorance".

7   Amartya Sen, *Identity and Violence: The Illusion of Destiny* (New Delhi: Penguin Books India, 2006).

8   Samuel Huntington, "If Not Civilizations, What? Paradigms of the Post-Cold War World," in *Foreign Affairs Presents the Clash of Civilizations? The Debate: Twentieth Anniversary Edition*, (Washington: Foreign Affairs, 2013), 64.

9   Huntington, "If Not Civilizations," 64.

10 Amina Chaudary, "The Clash of Civilizations Revisited," *Islamica Magazine*, http://www.digitalnpq.org/archive/2007_winter/14_huntington.html, accessed February 1, 2014.

11 Chaudary, "Clash Revisited."

MODULE 10
THE EVOLVING DEBATE

KEY POINTS

- 9/11 gave *Clash* heightened relevance because it seemed as though the "clash" between the West and Islam had now begun in earnest.

- *Clash* was a key text for neoconservatism,* a political ideology emphasizing muscular foreign policy and a pro-American stance.

- *Clash* informed neoclassical realism,* an academic discipline that rejects the "science" of neorealism* in favor of more "human" analysis.

Uses and Problems

Gideon Rose,* editor of *Foreign Affairs* and a former student of Samuel Huntington, charted the debate over the value of *The Clash of Civilizations.* "During the 1990s," Rose wrote, Samuel Huntington's thesis "was often attacked, with critics claiming that its intellectual framework obscured rather than clarified global trends, and that its vision of civilization had become a self-fulfilling prophecy."[1] On the other hand, in the aftermath of 9/11 and in the context of the global "War on Terror,"* *The Clash of Civilizations* was praised as particularly insightful.[2]

Some thinkers who had previously criticized Huntington were brought around to his point of view by the 9/11 attacks. Fouad Ajami* wrote: "I had questioned Huntington's suggestion that civilizations could be found 'whole and intact, watertight under an eternal sky.' Furrows, I observed, run across civilizations, and the [Liberal Democratic Western] consensus would hold in places

> **❝** Those 19 young Arabs who struck America on 9/11* were to give Huntington more of history's compliance than he could ever have imagined. He had written of a 'youth bulge' unsettling Muslim societies, and young Arabs and Muslims were now the shock-troops of a new radicalism. Their rise had overwhelmed the order in their homelands and had spilled into non-Muslim societies along the borders between Muslims and other peoples. Islam* had grown assertive and belligerent; the ideologies of Westernization that had dominated the histories of Turkey, Iran, and the Arab world, as well as South Asia, had faded. **❞**
>
> Fouad Ajami, "The Clash," in *The New York Times*

like India, Egypt, and Turkey," but "Huntington's thesis about a civilizational clash seems more compelling to me than the critique I provided at the time."[3]

Thanks to the firestorm of criticism that surrounded the publication of *Clash*, at first very few academics took up Huntington's project. Instead, the book influenced politicians, pundits, and those working to change public opinion. Ultimately, it wound up as a key text for an American political movement called neoconservatism—a group emphasizing the promotion of free markets and individual liberty around the world, and often criticized by Huntington himself.

Schools of Thought

Neoconservatism is a political ideology rather than an intellectual school, though the ideas in *Clash* are central to it. The great neoconservative international project of the post-9/11 era was the "War on Terror,"* which was largely based on Huntington's assumption that the West and Islam would inevitably come into conflict as long as they both existed. A centerpiece of the "War on Terror" was the 2003 American invasion and occupation of Iraq (the Iraq War).* The neoconservatives included National Security Advisor and then Secretary of State Condoleezza Rice,* Secretary of Defense Donald Rumsfeld,* and President George W. Bush.* They believed that America had to be protected from *potential* threats (the "Bush doctrine"), and so took the idea of a nuclear-armed Islamic Iraq (perceived, according to *Clash*, as intolerant of the existence of the West) as a serious threat to America and its interests. Huntington did not see himself as a neoconservative, however, and his relationship with neoconservatism was troubled at best. He was a vocal opponent of the invasion of Iraq, believing it to be little more than Western antagonism towards the Islamic world that would do more harm than good.[4]

In terms of its academic impact, *Clash* should be remembered as a founding text of neoclassical realism—the school of thought that believes state action can be explained by a combination of structural factors (such as the distribution of world power) and agent-driven factors (such as the ambitions of certain leaders). This is because Huntington wrote it partly as a criticism of neorealism—the belief that only structural factors determine how states behave. Huntington's 1993 article titled "The Clash of Civilizations?" was one of the first major works of realism* in the post-Cold War era, and one of the first to explicitly reject the scientific methodology of neorealism. Instead it shared the reflective tradition of the classical realists* such as Reinhold Niebuhr* and Hans Morgenthau.* Fareed Zakaria* and Gideon Rose disagree with the conclusions of *Clash*, but take a similar approach to realism in general. Rose wrote: "Neoclassical realists argue that relative material power establishes the basic parameters of a country's foreign policy," but went on to say that "foreign policy choices are made by actual leaders and elites, and so it is their perceptions of relative power that matter."

He added, importantly for Huntington, that they may not even be concerned with relative power, but rather with pride, anger, or fear.[5]

In Current Scholarship

Huntington's academic followers are a mixed bag. His former student Eliot Cohen* explained the lack of a distinct theoretical school based on his ideas by saying, "Sam's students are not a coherent band. We include hardheaded idealists and dreamy realists, bellicose liberals and pacifically inclined conservatives, even—gasp!—some neoconservatives."[6] Cohen emphasizes that the "school of Sam" was ultimately critical. Huntington taught his students at Harvard to challenge orthodoxy, rather than to follow any particular path.[7]

Fareed Zakaria,* who read for his PhD under Huntington, is perhaps his most notable disciple. In his book *The Post-American World*, Zakaria borrowed some concepts from Huntington, including that of the decline of the relative power of the West versus other civilizations. He wrote: "Some contemporary scholars, most famously Samuel P. Huntington, have argued that modernization and Westernization are wholly distinct . . . The West, Huntington argues, was Western before it was modern."[8] Zakaria, unlike Huntington, does not believe that modernization in the developing world will lead to clashes with the West. Instead, he argues that "rising powers appear to be following a third way." Rather than "integrating into the Western order . . . or becoming a rogue nation," rising powers are "moving from anger to indifference, from anti-Americanism [or pro-Americanism] to post-Americanism."[9]

NOTES

1 Gideon Rose, "Introduction," in *Foreign Affairs Presents the Clash of Civilizations? The Debate: Twentieth Anniversary Edition* (Washington: Foreign Affairs, 2013), 2.

2 Rose, "Introduction," 2.

3   Fouad Ajami, "The Clash," *New York Times*, http://www.nytimes. com/2008/01/06/books/review/Ajami-t.html?ref=samuelphuntington, accessed February 3, 2014.

4   Adam Sell, "Samuel Huntington, Author and Political Scientist, Dies," *New York Times*, http://www.nytimes.com/2008/12/28/world/ americas/28iht-obit.1.18954589.html, accessed February 5, 2014.

5   Gideon Rose, "Neoclassical Realism and Theories of Foreign Policy," *World Politics* 51, no. 1 (1998): 147.

6   Eliot Cohen, "The School of Sam," in *Foreign Affairs Presents the Clash of Civilizations? The Debate: Twentieth Anniversary Edition* (Washington: Foreign Affairs, 2013), 82.

7   Cohen, "School of Sam," 82-83.

8   Fareed Zakaria, *The Post American World* (New York: W.W. Norton and Company, 2008), 74.

9   Zakaria, *Post American*, 36.

MODULE 11
IMPACT AND INFLUENCE TODAY

KEY POINTS

- *Clash* still influences attitudes in American neoconservative* foreign policy, and the stance of anti-Islamic groups and authors.

- Taking their cues from *Clash*, neoconservatives suggest that Islam in the West ought to be confronted.

- Critics argue that describing "battle lines" between civilizations and defining divisions by culture smacks of orientalism* by the West.

Position

The Clash of Civilizations by Samuel Huntington remains an important text in modern politics, but it has not remained central to the discipline of international relations. The best way to understand the continued significance of a book like *Clash* is to return to Richard Betts'* description. "Its continued importance," Betts argues, "is not through ongoing academic debate, but rather, as a political [beacon] because even practical policymakers who shun ivory-tower theories still [may think roughly in terms of it]."[1]

Samuel Huntington's worldview was used to help define the broad political opinions of world leaders. This is to suggest not that leaders consulted Huntington's model before making decisions, but that his notion of "civilization" as an important force in politics has not gone away. "The United States is not at war with Islam," President Barack Obama* said in a 2014 speech to the Turkish Parliament.[2] Obama rejected Huntington's "clash" theory, instead

> ❝ We know that there are plenty of Islamists*
> eager to murder Westerners, even cut off our heads
> in broad daylight. No one doubts that they'd use
> something more lethal than a rusty machete if given
> the opportunity. And so the success or failure of
> Obama's* grand strategic vision depends entirely on
> what our enemies do next. That's because they get a
> vote, and they vote 'nay'. ❞
> Jonah Goldberg, "Our Enemies Get a Vote," in the *National Review*

assuming that the West and Turkey could cooperate: "This is not where East and West divide—it is where they come together."[3]

Interaction

The work's continued challenge to theories of liberal universalism* and postcolonialism* emerges in the use of the rhetoric of *Clash* by the American neoconservative* policy establishment. This includes think tanks such as the American Enterprise Institute (AEI)* and the Middle East Forum (MEF).* For example, in an article entitled "Our Enemies Get a Vote," Jonah Goldberg* wrote, "We know there are plenty of Islamists eager to murder Westerners, even cut off our heads in broad daylight."[4] These voices are supported by popular Islamophobic* literature—for example, *While Europe Slept: How Radical Islam is Destroying the West from Within* by Bruce Bawer,* and *Londonistan: How Britain is Creating a Terror State Within* by Melanie Phillips.* Phillips claims that Islamic terrorism has "an ideology that has taken hold like a cancer, not just in the madrasas of Pakistan, but also in the streets," and that a "world war [is] being waged by clerical fascism against free societies."[5]

Huntington stated outright that these uses of his *Clash* theory of civilizational conflict were not what he had in mind when he wrote the book: "Both [the West and Islam] have divisions. Western countries collaborate with Muslim countries and vice versa. It's a mistake ... to think in terms of two homogeneous sides starkly confronting one another."[6]

The Continuing Debate

An important post-9/11* critic of *The Clash of Civilizations* was Fred Halliday.* He argued that Samuel Huntington obscured the real source of conflict, which was class rather than culture. In Halliday's book *The Middle East in International Relations*, he argued that dividing the Middle East from the West by culture was false. The real tension was between frail authoritarian* states and the societies that are growing discontented with their rule. "The dividing line," Halliday wrote, "of the post-Cold War world ran as much within Middle Eastern societies as along any international . . . fault line."[7] Volker Perthes* added to Halliday's conclusion, writing: "We must remember we are not in a clash of cultures . . . the real clash or cultural conflict takes place within the Arab-Islamic civilization." Perthes saw the battle as an ideological one, rather than one between abusive political authority and unruly societies yearning for liberation.[8] The fight, he argued, is between those within the Islamic world who support globalization and engagement with the West, and "reactionary Utopian*" radical Islamists.*[9] Halliday and Perthes suggest that *Clash* draws the battle lines between the wrong groups.

Regarding the debate over cultures, Deepa Kumar* and Alana Lentin* have argued that the real mistake is drawing battle lines at all. They argue that *Clash*, especially in the hands of American neoconservatives, is essentially orientalism—the West treating Eastern cultures as exotic or dangerous—disguised as international relations theory. As Kumar argued in *Islamophobia and the Politics of Empire*, after 9/11 the US foreign policy establishment issued "loud proclamations that 'Islamic terrorists' represented existential threats to the United States," and that "US policy was geared toward 'keeping Americans safe' from Muslim 'evildoers'. These claims fly in the face of reality."[10] Islamist organizations, Kumar claimed, emerge (with very rare exceptions) at a local level to deal with local concerns, and are raised up as combatants in the imagined "clash" as part of the rhetoric of neoconservatives to "cover their imperial* ambitions."[11] Alana Lentin approached the argument from a different angle, believing that "the prevalence of the 'clash of civilizations' discourse has given racism new legitimacy."[12] According to Lentin, "theories of the new racism . . . focus on culture rather than biology," and have been used to construct Islam as "the nexus of asylum seekers, illegal immigrants [and] terrorists—and Muslims [generally] are shown to blend into a single target seen as threatening the West."[13]

NOTES

1 Richard Betts, "Conflict or Cooperation?" *Foreign Affairs* 89, no. 6 (2010): 186.

2 Barack Obama, "Presidential Address to the Turkish Parliament," http://www. hurriyet.com.tr/english/domestic/11376661.asp, accessed January 31, 2014.

3 Obama, "Address to Turkish Parliament."

4 Jonah Goldberg, "Our Enemies Get A Vote," *American Enterprise Institute*, http://www.aei.org/article/foreign-and-defense-policy/terrorism/our-enemies-get-a-vote/, accessed February 5, 2014.

5 Melanie Philips, *Londonistan* (New York: Encounter Books, 2007), xiv.

6 Amina Chaudary, "The Clash of Civilizations Revisited," *Islamica Magazine*, http://www.digitalnpq.org/archive/2007_winter/14_huntington. html, accessed February 1, 2014.

7 Fred Halliday, *The Middle East in International Relations: Power, Politics, and Ideology* (New York: Cambridge University Press, 2005), 158.

8 Volker Perthes, "Is the Arab World Immune to Democracy?" *Survival: Global Politics and Strategy* 50, no. 6 (2009): 158.

9 Perthes, "Arab World," 158.

10 Deepa Kumar, *Islamophobia and the Politics of Empire* (London: Haymarket Books, 2012), 113.

11 Kumar, *Islamophobia*, 114.

12 Alana Lentin, "Imagining the West, Perceiving Race: Social Sciences and Political Imagination," in *The Politics of Imagination*, ed. Chiara Bottici and Benoît Challand (Oxford: Birkbeck Law Press, 2011), 109.

13 Alana Lentin, *Racism: A Beginner's Guide* (London: Oneworld Publications, 2008), vi.

MODULE 12
WHERE NEXT?

KEY POINTS

- *The Clash of Civilizations* continues to be influential within right-wing political movements.
- The book will remain a target for criticism by postcolonial* political scientists.
- Samuel Huntington's work remains one of the most powerful and controversial post-Cold War* theories of global politics.

Potential

Samuel Huntington's *The Clash of Civilizations* has been enduringly influential in the *practice* of politics, but has not been enduringly influential in the *study* of politics. *Clash* became famous for influencing the neoconservative* administration of President George W. Bush* in the aftermath of 9/11,* although the relationship between neoconservative policy and Huntington's book remained troubled. When President Barack Obama* took office in 2008 neoconservatism became a relic of the Bush era and this rhetoric has largely been softened in official speeches. The Trump Presidency has seen another about turn, with strong nationalistic sympathies. This has resulted in policies that some deem anti-islamic, such as the 2017 travel ban, popularly reffered to as the "Muslim Ban."[1]

Open discussion of the *Clash* thesis has largely been relegated to right-wing extremist groups such as the English Defence League* and Greece's Golden Dawn* party. In mainstream politics, the discussion of cultural "clash" has been more limited, and associated with talk about the assimilation of Muslims into Western culture.

❝ Sam was the kind of scholar that made Harvard a great university. People all over the world studied and debated his ideas. I believe that he was clearly one of the most influential political scientists of the last 50 years. **❞**

Henry Rosovsky, American economic historian, and Lewis P. and Linda L. Geyser University Professor Emeritus at Harvard University

British Prime Minister David Cameron,* for example, said that when "unacceptable views or practices have come up from someone who isn't white [namely, Muslims], we've been too cautious . . . to stand up to them," and also that the "hands-off tolerance" of Muslim beliefs being incompatible with liberalism must end.[2] By "hands-off tolerance," Cameron is referring to a politics of non-interference— for example, allowing arranged marriages because they are simply too politically difficult to stop.

Future Directions

The most interesting academic developments directly related to the central argument in *Clash* emerged not in support of Huntington's argument, but in relation to the response to it in postcolonialist literature. Postcolonial scholars have used Huntington as a theoretical opposition to their own beliefs. One such academic, Jocelyne Cesari,* referred directly to Huntington in her argument concerning the French debate over Muslim dress. "Huntington," she wrote, gave "a static version of Islamic civilization and a unique Muslim psyche which compels conformity to Islamic law at all times—as though Muslims were a species unto themselves."[3] In this sense, the most important school of thought to come out of *Clash* does not build on its ideas; rather, it reacts against them.

Summary

Gideon Rose,* a former student and personal admirer of Huntington, wrote of the 1993 article that first set out the *Clash* theory: "A good way to measure the power of a theory is to look at the scale and intensity and quality of the debate it provokes; on those grounds, 'Clash' made one of the most powerful theoretical contributions in recent generations."[4]

Huntington's *Clash* was one of three attempts by three different thinkers to create the new "grand theory" of International politics after the Cold War.* It is true that none of the theories— Francis Fukuyama's* triumphalist liberal universalism,* John Mearsheimer's* scientific neorealism,* or Huntington's own pessimistic civilizational theory—won out in their own right. Huntington's theory, however, has remained most prominent of the three. While it helped define the theoretical school of neoclassical realism,* students reading *Clash* hoping for an outline of the neoclassical realist project will be sorely disappointed. That is because *Clash* served, really, only as an inspiration to prominent neoclassical realists. Thinkers such as Gideon Rose and Fareed Zakaria* share much with the book's underlying theoretical methodology and focus—its reflective approach, its concern with security, and its concern with America's place in a post-Cold War world—but they do not share Huntington's theory of civilizations.

Instead, the book's enduring importance became clear in the aftermath of 9/11 and during the **"War on Terror,"*** where it became central to the logic of American foreign policy. This centrality, however, has not been without controversy. The book has been labeled as racist and Islamophobic.* The book's critics, most prominently Edward Said,* believe that the neoconservative policy establishment in the United States used the book's logic to turn the 9/11 attacks into the first shot in a war between civilizations.[5] In this sense, Huntington's book was a grim self-fulfilling prophecy.

NOTES

1   Office of the Press Secretary, The White House, "President Donald
    J. Trump Strengthens Security Standards For Travelling to America,"
    whitehouse.gov/the-presi-office/2017/09/24/President-donald-j-trump-
    strengthens-security-standards-travelling/, accessed December 2, 2017.

2   David Cameron, "PM's Speech at Munich Security Conference," http://
    webarchive.nationalarchives.gov.uk/20130109092234/http://number10.
    gov.uk/news/pms-speech-at-munich-security-conference/, accessed March
    3, 2014.

3   Jocelyne Cesari, "Islam in France: The Shaping of a Religious Minority,"
    in *Muslims in the West, from Sojourners to Citizens*, ed. Yvonne Haddad-
    Yazbeck, (Oxford: Oxford University Press, 2002), 36.

4   Gideon Rose, "Introduction," in *Foreign Affairs Presents the Clash of
    Civilizations? The Debate: Twentieth Anniversary Edition* (Washington:
    Foreign Affairs, 2013), 2.

5   Edward Said, "The Clash of Ignorance," *The Nation*, http://www.thenation.
    com/article/clash-ignorance, accessed February 1, 2014.

GLOSSARIES

GLOSSARY OF TERMS

American Enterprise Institute (est. 1938): American think tank prominent in the making and implementing of neoconservative policy.

Anarchy: state of leaderlessness; sovereign states are in an anarchic world because there is no sovereign authority *above* states, compelling them one way or another.

Authoritarianism: form of government characterized by the absolute obedience to authority; regimes tend to be autocratic "presidents for life," and deeply related to a cult of personality surrounding the leader.

Behavioralism: approach to political science that emerged in the mid-twentieth century in America. It emphasized an objective, quantitative, and scientific approach to explaining political and social behavior.

Capitalism: economic and political system in which a country's trade and industry are controlled by private owners for profit, rather than by the state (*OED*).

Christianity: a religion that is based on the teachings of Jesus Christ.

Central Intelligence Agency (CIA): the CIA is the main international intelligence-gathering organization of the United States. It has occasionally taken on more active roles abroad, and has been implicated with interfering in foreign governments.

Classical realism: school of international relations theory that assumes state action is agent-driven (that is, controlled by leaders, rather than by structural imperative) and identifies the inherent imperfections of human nature as the source of conflict.

Cold War (1947–91): period of tension between America and the Soviet Union. While the two countries never engaged in direct military conflict, they engaged in covert and proxy wars and espionage against one another.

Communism: political ideology that relies on the state ownership of the means of production, the collectivization of labor, and the abolition of social class. It was the ideology of the Soviet Union (1917–89) and was in contrast to free-market capitalism during the Cold War.

Confucianism: ethical, philosophical, and religious system derived from the teachings of the Chinese philosopher Confucius (551–479 B.C.E.). Confucianism focuses on the practical and venerates institutions (such as the family or laws) rather than a deity and an afterlife.

Conservatism: a political philosophy that aims to retain traditional institutions and ways of thinking, emphasizing the value of stability over reinvention.

East Asian Economic Caucus (1990): regional free-trade zone proposed by then-Malaysian Prime Minister Dr. Mahathir bin Mohamad that was never executed due in no small part to Japanese reluctance.

English Defence League: far-right street protest movement in England designed to combat Islamic immigration and counteract what it believes to be a growing Islamic influence in Britain.

Essentialism: belief that things have a set of characteristics that make them what they are, and that the task of science and philosophy is their discovery and expression; the doctrine that essence is prior to existence.

European Union (1992): family of institutions that govern the legal, economic, and political union of 28 European states.

Free world: the name the American-led bloc in the Cold War gave itself. States in the "free world" were characterized by (at least nominal) commitments to democracy, free markets, and opposition to communism.

Fundamentalism: A form of a religion, especially Islam or Protestant Christianity, that upholds belief in the strict, literal interpretation of scripture (*OED*).

Golden Dawn: far-right Greek political party focused on promoting anti-immigration policies. It has been described by its own leadership as nationalist and racist.

Gulf War (1990–1): regional war between the coalition forces (led by America) and Iraq. The conflict was sparked by the invasion of neighboring Kuwait by Iraqi forces.

Heterogeneity: Diverse in character or content (*OED*).

Humanism: A rationalist outlook or system of thought attaching prime importance to human rather than divine or supernatural matters (*OED*).

Imperialism: policy of extending a country's power and influence through colonization, use of military force, or other means (*OED*).

Iraq War (2003–11): armed conflict initially between Iraq and the United States, and then between a protracted insurgency and the United States. The justification for war was that the United States and its allies believed that Saddam Hussein, the then-leader of Iraq, was secretly building a stockpile of nuclear weapons.

Islamic civilization: Huntington believed "Islamic" civilization was defined by Muslim majority countries—from Morocco in East Africa, to Indonesia in Southeast Asia.

Islamism: a political ideology based on the idea that society should draw its institutions from the tradition of Islamic thought.

Islamophobia: dislike of or prejudice against Islam or Muslims, especially as a political force (*OED*).

League of Nations (1920–46): international organization founded in the aftermath of World War I. It is considered to be the precursor to the modern United Nations.

Liberalism: school of international relations theory that suggests that states can, and ultimately will, achieve peace and mutual cooperation.

Liberal universalism: school of thought that emerged after the Cold War was "won" by the West in 1989. It assumes that Western, liberal values are universal and objectively superior—all people not only want liberalism, according to this theory, but they deserve liberalism as a human right.

Middle East Forum (est. 1990): American (neo)conservative think tank focusing on promoting American objectives in the Middle East.

Monolithic: Of an organization or system—large, powerful, indivisible, and slow to change.

Muslim: A follower of the religion of Islam.

Mutually assured destruction: doctrine of nuclear weapons strategy dictating that the use of nuclear weapons by two sides pitted against each other will result in the complete annihilation of both sides. It is considered to be a strong disincentive to both players against attacking and disarming.

Neoclassical realism: combination of neorealism and classical realism. Its adherents hold that state action can be explained with reference to both structural factors (such as the distribution of capabilities between states) and agent-driven factors (such as the ambitions of given leaders).

Neoconservatism: American political movement that emphasizes proactive promotion of free markets and individual liberty around the world.

Neoliberalism: school of international relations theory that holds that interstate cooperation is possible and likely, especially through international institutions, because states prefer to maximize their absolute welfare gains, rather than their relative security gains over one another.

Neorealism: school of international relations theory that assumes that structural constraints (such as anarchy and the distribution of world power), rather than human agency, will determine actors' behavior.

9/11: On September 11, 2001, four coordinated terror attacks were launched against America by the Islamic extremist group al-Qaeda. Four passenger airplanes were flown into various targets around the country, including the World Trade Center in New York City, and the Pentagon. The death toll of 2,977 civilians made it the largest attack against America in modern history.

Non-Aligned movement: a group of states that are not formally aligned with any power bloc. Jawaharlal Nehru, India's first prime minister, conceived of the bloc as a way for states to avoid domination by either America or the Soviet Union.

North Atlantic Treaty Organization (NATO): a collective defense organization comprised of 28 states. It is generally considered to be engaged in the promotion of American, or Western, interests abroad.

Orientalism: a term (coined by Edward Said in his 1978 book *Orientalism*) to describe the depiction of Eastern cultures by Western media as exotic, other, or dangerous.

Orthodox Civilization: Huntington believed "Orthodox" civilization was roughly defined by Russia and certain parts of Eastern Europe (such as Eastern Ukraine or Belarus).

Paradigm: worldview underlying the theories and methodology of a particular scientific subject (*OED*).

Polarity: the distribution of power within the international system—a bipolar system has power concentrated in two states, whereas a multipolar system has power concentrated in multiple states.

Postcolonial theory: academic discipline that focuses on analyzing, explaining, and exposing the cultural legacies of colonialism and imperialism.

Realism: school of international relations theory that assumes that: (1) states are the primary actors; (2) states all share the goal of survival; (3) states provide for their own security.

Reductivism: the practice of analyzing and describing a complex phenomenon in terms of its simple or fundamental constituents, especially when this is said to provide a sufficient explanation (*OED*).

Sinic civilization: Huntington believed "Sinic" civilization was defined by China and its near-abroad.

Soviet Union: a kind of "super state" that existed from 1922 to 1991, centered primarily on Russia and its neighbors. It was the communist pole of the Cold War.

States-as-billiard-balls: the billiard ball model in international relations theory suggests that states are akin to "billiard balls," inasmuch as they are all roughly the same and act only in relation to external forces. This model suggests that the internal politics of states are unimportant to understanding international relations. It is critical to neorealist theory.

Third World: the developing countries of Asia, Africa, and Latin America (*OED*).

Transition paradigm: the now largely discredited approach to democratization that assumes that all political openings lead to democracy, that democratization proceeds in set stages, that elections are of primary and singular importance, and that there are no institutional or developmental preconditions to democracy.

Utopia: An imagined place or state of things in which everything is perfect (*OED*).

War on Terror: the term commonly applied to American-led actions throughout the Middle East against non-state "terrorist" actors, including al-Qaeda. The drone campaign in Pakistan, the occupation of Afghanistan, and other covert and overt operations are rolled into this effort.

Warsaw Treaty Organization (WTO): the WTO was a collective defense organization led by the Soviet Union. It was formed in 1955, and dissolved in 1991 with the end of the Cold War.

Western Civilization: Huntington defined "the West" as America, Europe, and Oceania (Australia and New Zealand).

World War II (1939–45): global war between the vast majority of states, including all the great powers of the time.

Yugoslav Wars (1991–2001): a series of wars fought in southeastern Europe's Balkan peninsula between the successor states to the former Yugoslavia, including Serbia and Montenegro, Bosnia and Herzegovina, Kosovo, Croatia, and Slovenia.

PEOPLE MENTIONED IN THE TEXT

Fouad Ajami (1945–2014) was a Lebanese-American scholar on Middle Eastern Studies at Stanford University. Ajami became an outspoken supporter of American intervention in Iraq in 2003.

Bruce Bawer (b. 1956) is an American writer and activist. He is both a cultural critic, and poet who is a notable advocate of gay rights, and critic of radical Islam.

Isaiah Berlin (1909–97) was a Russian-British social and political theorist specializing in the history of ideas. While Berlin authored several seminal works, his most famous contributions have to do with how to understand liberty—is it "freedom from" or "freedom to"?

Richard Betts (b. 1947) is an American professor of international relations and security at Columbia University, and a senior fellow of the Council of Foreign Relations. His academic specialty is in strategy, intelligence, and military history, but he also works extensively with the American government.

Hedley Bull (1932–85) was Professor of International Relations at Australian National University, as well as at the London School of Economics and Oxford University. He is most famous as an "English School" theorist of international relations.

George W. Bush (b. 1946) was 43rd President of the United States from 2001 to 2009. The attacks of September 11, 2001, the invasion of Iraq in 2003, and the ongoing occupation of Afghanistan occurred under his presidency.

David Cameron (b. 1966) is Prime Minister of the United Kingdom (2010–present, as of the writing of this analysis). His premiership involves serious skepticism on the viability of the European Union.

James "Jimmy" Carter (b. 1924) is an American politician who was the country's 39th President (1977–81). He won the Nobel Peace Prize in 2002.

Jocelyne Cesari is an American lecturer in Islamic Studies in the Faculty of Divinity at Harvard University. She specializes in engagement between the Islamic world and the West, especially in light of immigration and terror issues.

Eliot Cohen (b. 1956) is an American political science academic at Johns Hopkins University. While he specializes in strategic studies, especially strategy pertaining to American interests in the Middle East, he is also an active counselor to the American government.

Francis Fukuyama (b. 1952) is a Japanese-American professor of international relations at Stanford University. He is a well-known proponent of international liberalism, which refers to free markets, democratic elections, and Western secularism.

Jonah Goldberg (b. 1969) is an American conservative columnist and author. He is best known for his media presence, as well as his popular books, which are often anti-liberal in nature.

Fred Halliday (1946–2010) was an Irish academic specializing in the international relations of the Middle East and theories of revolution. Halliday, as one of the foremost British voices in both fields of study, was elected to the British Academy in 2002.

Robert Keohane (b. 1941) is an American political science professor at Princeton University. He is associated with neoliberalism and co-wrote *Power and Interdependence* with Joseph Nye. His first book, *After Hegemony*, is considered foundational in neoliberal theory.

Gilles Kepel (b. 1955) is a French political scientist at Sciences Po in Paris, specializing in Islamic Studies. He argues that Muslim extremists should be seen as external to Islam in general, and that Muslim civilians often oppose violent attacks.

Deepa Kumar (b. 1968) is joint Professor of Media Studies and Middle Eastern Studies at Rutgers University in the United States. She argues, in general, that Western authorities have painted Muslims as threatening since the Crusades in the eleventh century.

Imre Lakatos (1922–74) was a Hungarian philosopher of math and science. He was notable for his thought on methodology in the social sciences and for introducing the concept of a "research program." This idea contends that each theory has a "hard core" proposition that makes it distinctive and that should not be revised, as well as malleable theories around the "hard core" that should be altered to keep the theory current.

Alana Lentin is a social theorist currently teaching at the University of Sussex in the UK. She specializes in theories of race and cultural engagement, and the ways in which the meaning and political significance of "race" has changed over time.

Bernard Lewis (b. 1916) is a British-American historian specializing in oriental studies He is the Cleveland E. Dodge Professor Emeritus of Near Eastern Studies at Princeton University. Lewis is known for his controversial view that the Middle East is "backward," and that its backwardness is largely "self inflicted" by Islamic culture and religion.

John Mearsheimer (b. 1947) is an American international relations professor and neorealist. He is the pioneer of "offensive realism," a contemporary reformulation of neorealism. Offensive realists believe that states will try to maximize their power relative to one another, rather than secure "just enough" to maintain security.

Hans Morgenthau (1904–80) was a German political theorist who worked primarily in America. He has been described as the most prominent of the classical realists. Morgenthau advanced the classical realist position that global politics was defined by the flawed, power-hungry nature of humanity, rather than by the dispassionate calculations of abstract "state" entities.

Reinhold Niebuhr (1892–1971) was an American theology professor who was highly influential in public affairs. He wrote that humankind's sinful, wicked, and irrational nature made international peace impossible. He is often seen as part of the classical realist tradition.

Joseph Nye (b. 1937) is an American political science professor at Harvard. He co-wrote *Power and Interdependence* with Robert Keohane, effectively helping found neoliberalism. He is also considered to be the father of theories of "complex interdependence," which illustrate how states will avoid conflict with other states when their interests are bound up with each other's success.

Barack Obama (b. 1961) is the 44th President of the United States. His administration, in addition to carrying out many domestic reforms, is credited with reducing the American military presence in the Middle East.

Minxin Pei (b. 1957) is a Chinese-American political scientist who teaches international relations at Claremont-McKenna College. He specializes in the government of the People's Republic of China, and often writes on the subject for the Carnegie Endowment.

Volker Perthes (b. 1958) is the director of the German Institute for International and Security Affairs. Perthes specializes in the study of European–Middle Eastern engagement and sources of instability in the region.

Melanie Phillips (b. 1951) is a British journalist, author, and right-wing pundit. Due to her controversial views on immigration, she has been accused of Islamophobia—she has often argued that Islam poses a threat to Western societies.

Condoleezza Rice (b. 1954) was National Security Advisor (2001–5) and Secretary of State (2005–9) under George W. Bush. As one of the architects of, among other projects, the Iraq War, she is seen as a prominent neoconservative.

Gideon Rose is an American professor and policy advisor in international relations at Colombia University, and has edited *Foreign Affairs* magazine since 2010. He was a member of former President Bill Clinton's administration, and served on the National Security Council from 1994 to 1995.

Donald Rumsfeld (b. 1932) is an American politician and businessman. He has served as Secretary of Defense twice—first under Gerald Ford (1975–7) and then under George W. Bush (2001–6). He is known as an architect of both the Iraq War and the "War on Terror."

Edward Said (1935–2003) was a Palestinian-American scholar, public intellectual, and early postcolonial theorist. His *Orientalism* (1978) critiqued the ways in which the West perceived and represented the East.

Amartya Sen (b. 1933) is an Indian economist and Nobel laureate (awarded the Nobel Prize in 1998 for his work on welfare economics) who has been associated with Oxford, Harvard, and Cambridge. He is known as the pioneer of the "capability approach" to economic development, which holds that "development" should be seen not in purely economic terms, but in terms of what people can actually "do and be."

Kenneth Waltz (1924–2013) was an American international relations professor best known for reformulating realism in order to make it more scientific (the reformulation often being called neorealism). Neorealism, which argued that states are naturally suspicious of one another and prone to secure their position by balancing power, was the dominant theory of international relations from the 1970s to the 1990s.

Woodrow Wilson (1856–1924) was the 28th President of the United States. He is notable for presiding over the country during World War I (1914–18) and for helping restore international order in the aftermath.

Fareed Zakaria (b. 1964) is an Indian-American journalist and author. He has been managing editor of *Foreign Affairs* and *Time*, and notably authored *The Post-American World*. He believes that America's importance has declined, but that it is in no danger from countries that are largely "over" an American-dominated world.

WORKS CITED

WORKS CITED

Ajami, Fouad. "The Summoning." *Foreign Affairs* 72, no. 4 (1993): 2–9.

_____. "The Clash." *New York Times.* Accessed February 3, 2014. http://www.nytimes.com/2008/01/06/books/review/Ajami-t.html?ref=samuelphuntington.

Berlin, Isaiah. *The Hedgehog and the Fox: An Essay on Tolstoy's View of History.* New York: Simon and Schuster, 1986.

Betts, Richard. "Conflict or Cooperation?" *Foreign Affairs* 89, no. 6 (2010): 186–94.

Bush, George. "Address to the Nation on September 11th, 2001." *Washington Post.* Accessed February 1, 2014. http://www.washingtonpost.com/wp-dyn/content/article/2006/09/11/AR2006091100775.html.

Cameron, David. "PM's Speech at Munich Security Conference." Accessed March 3, 2014. http://webarchive.nationalarchives.gov.uk/20130109092234/http://number10.gov.uk/news/pms-speech-at-munich-security-conference/.

Cesari, Jocelyne. "Islam in France: The Shaping of a Religious Minority." In *Muslims in the West, from Sojourners to Citizens*, edited by Yvonne Haddad-Yazbeck, 36–52. Oxford: Oxford University Press, 2002.

Chaudary, Amina. "The Clash of Civilizations Revisited," *Islamica Magazine.* Accessed February 1, 2014. http://www.digitalnpq.org/archive/2007_winter/14_huntington.html.

Cohen, Eliot. "The School of Sam." In *Foreign Affairs Presents the Clash of Civilizations? The Debate: Twentieth Anniversary Edition*, 82–4. Washington: Foreign Affairs, 2013.

Fukuyama, Francis. "The End of History?" *The National Interest*, Summer (1989): 5.

Goldberg, Jonah. "Our Enemies Get A Vote." *American Enterprise Institute.* Accessed February 5, 2014. http://www.aei.org/article/foreign-and-defense-policy/terrorism/our-enemies-get-a-vote/.

Halliday, Fred. *The Middle East in International Relations: Power, Politics, and Ideology.* New York: Cambridge University Press, 2005.

Hodgson, Godfrey. "Obituary: Samuel Huntington." *The Guardian.* Accessed January 29, 2014. http://www.theguardian.com/world/2009/jan/01/obituary-samuel-huntington.

Huntington, Samuel. *Political Order in Changing Societies.* New Haven: Yale University Press, 1968.

_____, *The Soldier and the State*. Cambridge: Belknap Press, 1981.

_____. *The Third Wave: Democratization in the Late Twentieth Century*. Norman: University of Oklahoma Press, 1991.

_____, "Democracy's Third Wave," *Journal of Democracy* 2, no. 2 (1991): 12–34.

_____, "The Clash of Civilizations?" *Foreign Affairs* 72, no. 3 (1993): 22–49.

_____, *The Clash of Civilizations and the Remaking of World Order*. London: Simon and Schuster, 2002.

_____, "If Not Civilizations, What? Paradigms of the Post-Cold War World." In *Foreign Affairs Presents the Clash of Civilizations? The Debate: Twentieth Anniversary Edition*, compiled by Gideon Rose, 58–69. Washington: Foreign Affairs, 2013.

Ireland, Corydon. "Obituaries: Samuel Huntington, 81, Political Scientist, Scholar." *Harvard Gazette*. Accessed January 29, 2014. http://news.harvard.edu/gazette/story/2009/02/samuel-huntington-81-political-scientist-scholar/.

Kaplan, Robert. "Looking the World in the Eye." *The Atlantic*. Accessed January 29, 2014. http://www.theatlantic.com/magazine/archive/2001/12/looking-the-world-in-the-eye/302354/

Keohane, Robert, and Joseph Nye. *After Hegemony: Cooperation and Discord in the World Political Economy*. Princeton: Princeton University Press, 1984.

Kepel, Gilles. *The Revenge of God: The Resurgence of Islam, Christianity, and Judaism in the Modern World*. Translated by Alan Bradley. University Park: Pennsylvania State University Press, 1993.

Kumar, Deepa. *Islamophobia and the Politics of Empire*. London: Haymarket Books, 2012.

Lamy, Paul, Victory Armony, and André Tremblay. "Values, Culture, and Economic Integration: An Empirical Perspective on Culturalist Approaches." *Diálogos Latinamericanos* 9 (2004): 87–102.

Lentin, Alana. *Racism: A Beginner's Guide*. London: Oneworld Publications, 2008, vi.

_____, "Imagining the West, Perceiving Race: Social Sciences and Political Imagination." In *The Politics of Imagination*, edited by Chiara Bottici and Benoît Challand, 109–24. Oxford: Birkbeck Law Press, 2011.

Lewis, Bernard. "The Roots of Muslim Rage." *The Atlantic* 226, no. 3 (1990): 47.

Mearsheimer, John. "The Case for a Ukranian Nuclear Deterrent." *Foreign Affairs* 72 (1993): 50–66.

Morgenthau, Hans. *Politics Among Nations*. New York: McGraw Hill, 1979.

Niebuhr, Reinhold. *The Irony of American History*. London: Nisbet & Co, 1952, 113–14.

Obama, Barack. "Presidential Address to the Turkish Parliament." Accessed January 31, 2014. http://www.hurriyet.com.tr/english/domestic/11376661.asp.

Pei, Minxin. quoted in Katherine Yester, "Samuel Huntington, 1927–2008." *Foreign Policy*. Accessed January 30, 2014. http://www.foreignpolicy.com/articles/2009/02/16/samuel_huntington_1927_2008.

Perthes, Volker. "Is the Arab World Immune to Democracy?" *Survival: Global Politics and Strategy* 50, no. 6 (2009): 151–60.

Philips, Melanie. *Londonistan*. New York: Encounter Books, 2007.

Rose, Gideon. "Neoclassical Realism and Theories of Foreign Policy." *World Politics* 51, no. 1 (1998): 144–72.

_____, Introduction to *Foreign Affairs Presents the Clash of Civilizations? The Debate: Twentieth Anniversary Edition*, 1–3. Washington: Foreign Affairs, 2013.

Said, Edward. "The Clash of Ignorance," *The Nation*. Accessed February 1, 2014. http://www.thenation.com/article/clash-ignorance.

_____, "Transcript of The Myth of the Clash of Civilizations," *Media Education Foundation*. http://www.mediaed.org/assets/products/404/transcript_404.pdf

Sell, Adam. "Samuel Huntington, Author and Political Scientist, Dies." *New York Times*. Accessed February 5, 2014. http://www.nytimes.com/2008/12/28/world/americas/28iht-obit.1.18954589.html.

Sen, Amartya. *Identity and Violence: The Illusion of Destiny.* New Delhi: Penguin Books India, 2006.

Walt, Stephen. "International Relations: One World, Many Theories," *Foreign Policy* 110 (1998): 29–32, 34–46.

Waltz, Kenneth. *Theory of International Politics*. Reading: Addison Wesley, 1979.

Zakaria, Fareed. *The Post American World*. New York: W.W. Norton and Company, 2008.

THE MACAT LIBRARY
BY DISCIPLINE

AFRICANA STUDIES

Chinua Achebe's *An Image of Africa: Racism in Conrad's Heart of Darkness*
W. E. B. Du Bois's *The Souls of Black Folk*
Zora Neale Huston's *Characteristics of Negro Expression*
Martin Luther King Jr's *Why We Can't Wait*
Toni Morrison's *Playing in the Dark: Whiteness in the American Literary Imagination*

ANTHROPOLOGY

Arjun Appadurai's *Modernity at Large: Cultural Dimensions of Globalisation*
Philippe Ariès's *Centuries of Childhood*
Franz Boas's *Race, Language and Culture*
Kim Chan & Renée Mauborgne's *Blue Ocean Strategy*
Jared Diamond's *Guns, Germs & Steel: the Fate of Human Societies*
Jared Diamond's *Collapse: How Societies Choose to Fail or Survive*
E. E. Evans-Pritchard's *Witchcraft, Oracles and Magic Among the Azande*
James Ferguson's *The Anti-Politics Machine*
Clifford Geertz's *The Interpretation of Cultures*
David Graeber's *Debt: the First 5000 Years*
Karen Ho's *Liquidated: An Ethnography of Wall Street*
Geert Hofstede's *Culture's Consequences: Comparing Values, Behaviors, Institutes and Organizations across Nations*
Claude Lévi-Strauss's *Structural Anthropology*
Jay Macleod's *Ain't No Makin' It: Aspirations and Attainment in a Low-Income Neighborhood*
Saba Mahmood's *The Politics of Piety: The Islamic Revival and the Feminist Subject*
Marcel Mauss's *The Gift*

BUSINESS

Jean Lave & Etienne Wenger's *Situated Learning*
Theodore Levitt's *Marketing Myopia*
Burton G. Malkiel's *A Random Walk Down Wall Street*
Douglas McGregor's *The Human Side of Enterprise*
Michael Porter's *Competitive Strategy: Creating and Sustaining Superior Performance*
John Kotter's *Leading Change*
C. K. Prahalad & Gary Hamel's *The Core Competence of the Corporation*

CRIMINOLOGY

Michelle Alexander's *The New Jim Crow: Mass Incarceration in the Age of Colorblindness*
Michael R. Gottfredson & Travis Hirschi's *A General Theory of Crime*
Richard Herrnstein & Charles A. Murray's *The Bell Curve: Intelligence and Class Structure in American Life*
Elizabeth Loftus's *Eyewitness Testimony*
Jay Macleod's *Ain't No Makin' It: Aspirations and Attainment in a Low-Income Neighborhood*
Philip Zimbardo's *The Lucifer Effect*

ECONOMICS

Janet Abu-Lughod's *Before European Hegemony*
Ha-Joon Chang's *Kicking Away the Ladder*
David Brion Davis's *The Problem of Slavery in the Age of Revolution*
Milton Friedman's *The Role of Monetary Policy*
Milton Friedman's *Capitalism and Freedom*
David Graeber's *Debt: the First 5000 Years*
Friedrich Hayek's *The Road to Serfdom*
Karen Ho's *Liquidated: An Ethnography of Wall Street*

John Maynard Keynes's *The General Theory of Employment, Interest and Money*
Charles P. Kindleberger's *Manias, Panics and Crashes*
Robert Lucas's *Why Doesn't Capital Flow from Rich to Poor Countries?*
Burton G. Malkiel's *A Random Walk Down Wall Street*
Thomas Robert Malthus's *An Essay on the Principle of Population*
Karl Marx's *Capital*
Thomas Piketty's *Capital in the Twenty-First Century*
Amartya Sen's *Development as Freedom*
Adam Smith's *The Wealth of Nations*
Nassim Nicholas Taleb's *The Black Swan: The Impact of the Highly Improbable*
Amos Tversky's & Daniel Kahneman's *Judgment under Uncertainty: Heuristics and Biases*
Mahbub Ul Haq's *Reflections on Human Development*
Max Weber's *The Protestant Ethic and the Spirit of Capitalism*

FEMINISM AND GENDER STUDIES

Judith Butler's *Gender Trouble*
Simone De Beauvoir's *The Second Sex*
Michel Foucault's *History of Sexuality*
Betty Friedan's *The Feminine Mystique*
Saba Mahmood's *The Politics of Piety: The Islamic Revival and the Feminist Subject*
Joan Wallach Scott's *Gender and the Politics of History*
Mary Wollstonecraft's *A Vindication of the Rights of Woman*
Virginia Woolf's *A Room of One's Own*

GEOGRAPHY

The Brundtland Report's *Our Common Future*
Rachel Carson's *Silent Spring*
Charles Darwin's *On the Origin of Species*
James Ferguson's *The Anti-Politics Machine*
Jane Jacobs's *The Death and Life of Great American Cities*
James Lovelock's *Gaia: A New Look at Life on Earth*
Amartya Sen's *Development as Freedom*
Mathis Wackernagel & William Rees's *Our Ecological Footprint*

HISTORY

Janet Abu-Lughod's *Before European Hegemony*
Benedict Anderson's *Imagined Communities*
Bernard Bailyn's *The Ideological Origins of the American Revolution*
Hanna Batatu's *The Old Social Classes And The Revolutionary Movements Of Iraq*
Christopher Browning's *Ordinary Men: Reserve Police Batallion 101 and the Final Solution in Poland*
Edmund Burke's *Reflections on the Revolution in France*
William Cronon's *Nature's Metropolis: Chicago And The Great West*
Alfred W. Crosby's *The Columbian Exchange*
Hamid Dabashi's *Iran: A People Interrupted*
David Brion Davis's *The Problem of Slavery in the Age of Revolution*
Nathalie Zemon Davis's *The Return of Martin Guerre*
Jared Diamond's *Guns, Germs & Steel: the Fate of Human Societies*
Frank Dikotter's *Mao's Great Famine*
John W Dower's *War Without Mercy: Race And Power In The Pacific War*
W. E. B. Du Bois's *The Souls of Black Folk*
Richard J. Evans's *In Defence of History*
Lucien Febvre's *The Problem of Unbelief in the 16th Century*
Sheila Fitzpatrick's *Everyday Stalinism*

Eric Foner's *Reconstruction: America's Unfinished Revolution, 1863-1877*
Michel Foucault's *Discipline and Punish*
Michel Foucault's *History of Sexuality*
Francis Fukuyama's *The End of History and the Last Man*
John Lewis Gaddis's *We Now Know: Rethinking Cold War History*
Ernest Gellner's *Nations and Nationalism*
Eugene Genovese's *Roll, Jordan, Roll: The World the Slaves Made*
Carlo Ginzburg's *The Night Battles*
Daniel Goldhagen's *Hitler's Willing Executioners*
Jack Goldstone's *Revolution and Rebellion in the Early Modern World*
Antonio Gramsci's *The Prison Notebooks*
Alexander Hamilton, John Jay & James Madison's *The Federalist Papers*
Christopher Hill's *The World Turned Upside Down*
Carole Hillenbrand's *The Crusades: Islamic Perspectives*
Thomas Hobbes's *Leviathan*
Eric Hobsbawm's *The Age Of Revolution*
John A. Hobson's *Imperialism: A Study*
Albert Hourani's *History of the Arab Peoples*
Samuel P. Huntington's *The Clash of Civilizations and the Remaking of World Order*
C. L. R. James's *The Black Jacobins*
Tony Judt's *Postwar: A History of Europe Since 1945*
Ernst Kantorowicz's *The King's Two Bodies: A Study in Medieval Political Theology*
Paul Kennedy's *The Rise and Fall of the Great Powers*
Ian Kershaw's *The "Hitler Myth": Image and Reality in the Third Reich*
John Maynard Keynes's *The General Theory of Employment, Interest and Money*
Charles P. Kindleberger's *Manias, Panics and Crashes*
Martin Luther King Jr's *Why We Can't Wait*
Henry Kissinger's *World Order: Reflections on the Character of Nations and the Course of History*
Thomas Kuhn's *The Structure of Scientific Revolutions*
Georges Lefebvre's *The Coming of the French Revolution*
John Locke's *Two Treatises of Government*
Niccolò Machiavelli's *The Prince*
Thomas Robert Malthus's *An Essay on the Principle of Population*
Mahmood Mamdani's *Citizen and Subject: Contemporary Africa And The Legacy Of Late Colonialism*
Karl Marx's *Capital*
Stanley Milgram's *Obedience to Authority*
John Stuart Mill's *On Liberty*
Thomas Paine's *Common Sense*
Thomas Paine's *Rights of Man*
Geoffrey Parker's *Global Crisis: War, Climate Change and Catastrophe in the Seventeenth Century*
Jonathan Riley-Smith's *The First Crusade and the Idea of Crusading*
Jean-Jacques Rousseau's *The Social Contract*
Joan Wallach Scott's *Gender and the Politics of History*
Theda Skocpol's *States and Social Revolutions*
Adam Smith's *The Wealth of Nations*
Timothy Snyder's *Bloodlands: Europe Between Hitler and Stalin*
Sun Tzu's *The Art of War*
Keith Thomas's *Religion and the Decline of Magic*
Thucydides's *The History of the Peloponnesian War*
Frederick Jackson Turner's *The Significance of the Frontier in American History*
Odd Arne Westad's *The Global Cold War: Third World Interventions And The Making Of Our Times*

LITERATURE

Chinua Achebe's *An Image of Africa: Racism in Conrad's Heart of Darkness*
Roland Barthes's *Mythologies*
Homi K. Bhabha's *The Location of Culture*
Judith Butler's *Gender Trouble*
Simone De Beauvoir's *The Second Sex*
Ferdinand De Saussure's *Course in General Linguistics*
T. S. Eliot's *The Sacred Wood: Essays on Poetry and Criticism*
Zora Neale Huston's *Characteristics of Negro Expression*
Toni Morrison's *Playing in the Dark: Whiteness in the American Literary Imagination*
Edward Said's *Orientalism*
Gayatri Chakravorty Spivak's *Can the Subaltern Speak?*
Mary Wollstonecraft's *A Vindication of the Rights of Women*
Virginia Woolf's *A Room of One's Own*

PHILOSOPHY

Elizabeth Anscombe's *Modern Moral Philosophy*
Hannah Arendt's *The Human Condition*
Aristotle's *Metaphysics*
Aristotle's *Nicomachean Ethics*
Edmund Gettier's *Is Justified True Belief Knowledge?*
Georg Wilhelm Friedrich Hegel's *Phenomenology of Spirit*
David Hume's *Dialogues Concerning Natural Religion*
David Hume's *The Enquiry for Human Understanding*
Immanuel Kant's *Religion within the Boundaries of Mere Reason*
Immanuel Kant's *Critique of Pure Reason*
Søren Kierkegaard's *The Sickness Unto Death*
Søren Kierkegaard's *Fear and Trembling*
C. S. Lewis's *The Abolition of Man*
Alasdair MacIntyre's *After Virtue*
Marcus Aurelius's *Meditations*
Friedrich Nietzsche's *On the Genealogy of Morality*
Friedrich Nietzsche's *Beyond Good and Evil*
Plato's *Republic*
Plato's *Symposium*
Jean-Jacques Rousseau's *The Social Contract*
Gilbert Ryle's *The Concept of Mind*
Baruch Spinoza's *Ethics*
Sun Tzu's *The Art of War*
Ludwig Wittgenstein's *Philosophical Investigations*

POLITICS

Benedict Anderson's *Imagined Communities*
Aristotle's *Politics*
Bernard Bailyn's *The Ideological Origins of the American Revolution*
Edmund Burke's *Reflections on the Revolution in France*
John C. Calhoun's *A Disquisition on Government*
Ha-Joon Chang's *Kicking Away the Ladder*
Hamid Dabashi's *Iran: A People Interrupted*
Hamid Dabashi's *Theology of Discontent: The Ideological Foundation of the Islamic Revolution in Iran*
Robert Dahl's *Democracy and its Critics*
Robert Dahl's *Who Governs?*
David Brion Davis's *The Problem of Slavery in the Age of Revolution*

The Macat Library By Discipline

Alexis De Tocqueville's *Democracy in America*
James Ferguson's *The Anti-Politics Machine*
Frank Dikotter's *Mao's Great Famine*
Sheila Fitzpatrick's *Everyday Stalinism*
Eric Foner's *Reconstruction: America's Unfinished Revolution, 1863-1877*
Milton Friedman's *Capitalism and Freedom*
Francis Fukuyama's *The End of History and the Last Man*
John Lewis Gaddis's *We Now Know: Rethinking Cold War History*
Ernest Gellner's *Nations and Nationalism*
David Graeber's *Debt: the First 5000 Years*
Antonio Gramsci's *The Prison Notebooks*
Alexander Hamilton, John Jay & James Madison's *The Federalist Papers*
Friedrich Hayek's *The Road to Serfdom*
Christopher Hill's *The World Turned Upside Down*
Thomas Hobbes's *Leviathan*
John A. Hobson's *Imperialism: A Study*
Samuel P. Huntington's *The Clash of Civilizations and the Remaking of World Order*
Tony Judt's *Postwar: A History of Europe Since 1945*
David C. Kang's *China Rising: Peace, Power and Order in East Asia*
Paul Kennedy's *The Rise and Fall of Great Powers*
Robert Keohane's *After Hegemony*
Martin Luther King Jr.'s *Why We Can't Wait*
Henry Kissinger's *World Order: Reflections on the Character of Nations and the Course of History*
John Locke's *Two Treatises of Government*
Niccolò Machiavelli's *The Prince*
Thomas Robert Malthus's *An Essay on the Principle of Population*
Mahmood Mamdani's *Citizen and Subject: Contemporary Africa And The Legacy Of Late Colonialism*
Karl Marx's *Capital*
John Stuart Mill's *On Liberty*
John Stuart Mill's *Utilitarianism*
Hans Morgenthau's *Politics Among Nations*
Thomas Paine's *Common Sense*
Thomas Paine's *Rights of Man*
Thomas Piketty's *Capital in the Twenty-First Century*
Robert D. Putman's *Bowling Alone*
John Rawls's *Theory of Justice*
Jean-Jacques Rousseau's *The Social Contract*
Theda Skocpol's *States and Social Revolutions*
Adam Smith's *The Wealth of Nations*
Sun Tzu's *The Art of War*
Henry David Thoreau's *Civil Disobedience*
Thucydides's *The History of the Peloponnesian War*
Kenneth Waltz's *Theory of International Politics*
Max Weber's *Politics as a Vocation*
Odd Arne Westad's *The Global Cold War: Third World Interventions And The Making Of Our Times*

POSTCOLONIAL STUDIES

Roland Barthes's *Mythologies*
Frantz Fanon's *Black Skin, White Masks*
Homi K. Bhabha's *The Location of Culture*
Gustavo Gutiérrez's *A Theology of Liberation*
Edward Said's *Orientalism*
Gayatri Chakravorty Spivak's *Can the Subaltern Speak?*

PSYCHOLOGY

Gordon Allport's *The Nature of Prejudice*
Alan Baddeley & Graham Hitch's *Aggression: A Social Learning Analysis*
Albert Bandura's *Aggression: A Social Learning Analysis*
Leon Festinger's *A Theory of Cognitive Dissonance*
Sigmund Freud's *The Interpretation of Dreams*
Betty Friedan's *The Feminine Mystique*
Michael R. Gottfredson & Travis Hirschi's *A General Theory of Crime*
Eric Hoffer's *The True Believer: Thoughts on the Nature of Mass Movements*
William James's *Principles of Psychology*
Elizabeth Loftus's *Eyewitness Testimony*
A. H. Maslow's *A Theory of Human Motivation*
Stanley Milgram's *Obedience to Authority*
Steven Pinker's *The Better Angels of Our Nature*
Oliver Sacks's *The Man Who Mistook His Wife For a Hat*
Richard Thaler & Cass Sunstein's *Nudge: Improving Decisions About Health, Wealth and Happiness*
Amos Tversky's *Judgment under Uncertainty: Heuristics and Biases*
Philip Zimbardo's *The Lucifer Effect*

SCIENCE

Rachel Carson's *Silent Spring*
William Cronon's *Nature's Metropolis: Chicago And The Great West*
Alfred W. Crosby's *The Columbian Exchange*
Charles Darwin's *On the Origin of Species*
Richard Dawkin's *The Selfish Gene*
Thomas Kuhn's *The Structure of Scientific Revolutions*
Geoffrey Parker's *Global Crisis: War, Climate Change and Catastrophe in the Seventeenth Century*
Mathis Wackernagel & William Rees's *Our Ecological Footprint*

SOCIOLOGY

Michelle Alexander's *The New Jim Crow: Mass Incarceration in the Age of Colorblindness*
Gordon Allport's *The Nature of Prejudice*
Albert Bandura's *Aggression: A Social Learning Analysis*
Hanna Batatu's *The Old Social Classes And The Revolutionary Movements Of Iraq*
Ha-Joon Chang's *Kicking Away the Ladder*
W. E. B. Du Bois's *The Souls of Black Folk*
Émile Durkheim's *On Suicide*
Frantz Fanon's *Black Skin, White Masks*
Frantz Fanon's *The Wretched of the Earth*
Eric Foner's *Reconstruction: America's Unfinished Revolution, 1863-1877*
Eugene Genovese's *Roll, Jordan, Roll: The World the Slaves Made*
Jack Goldstone's *Revolution and Rebellion in the Early Modern World*
Antonio Gramsci's *The Prison Notebooks*
Richard Herrnstein & Charles A Murray's *The Bell Curve: Intelligence and Class Structure in American Life*
Eric Hoffer's *The True Believer: Thoughts on the Nature of Mass Movements*
Jane Jacobs's *The Death and Life of Great American Cities*
Robert Lucas's *Why Doesn't Capital Flow from Rich to Poor Countries?*
Jay Macleod's *Ain't No Makin' It: Aspirations and Attainment in a Low Income Neighborhood*
Elaine May's *Homeward Bound: American Families in the Cold War Era*
Douglas McGregor's *The Human Side of Enterprise*
C. Wright Mills's *The Sociological Imagination*

The Macat Library By Discipline

Thomas Piketty's *Capital in the Twenty-First Century*
Robert D. Putman's *Bowling Alone*
David Riesman's *The Lonely Crowd: A Study of the Changing American Character*
Edward Said's *Orientalism*
Joan Wallach Scott's *Gender and the Politics of History*
Theda Skocpol's *States and Social Revolutions*
Max Weber's *The Protestant Ethic and the Spirit of Capitalism*

THEOLOGY

Augustine's *Confessions*
Benedict's *Rule of St Benedict*
Gustavo Gutiérrez's *A Theology of Liberation*
Carole Hillenbrand's *The Crusades: Islamic Perspectives*
David Hume's *Dialogues Concerning Natural Religion*
Immanuel Kant's *Religion within the Boundaries of Mere Reason*
Ernst Kantorowicz's *The King's Two Bodies: A Study in Medieval Political Theology*
Søren Kierkegaard's *The Sickness Unto Death*
C. S. Lewis's *The Abolition of Man*
Saba Mahmood's *The Politics of Piety: The Islamic Revival and the Feminist Subject*
Baruch Spinoza's *Ethics*
Keith Thomas's *Religion and the Decline of Magic*

COMING SOON

Chris Argyris's *The Individual and the Organisation*
Seyla Benhabib's *The Rights of Others*
Walter Benjamin's *The Work Of Art in the Age of Mechanical Reproduction*
John Berger's *Ways of Seeing*
Pierre Bourdieu's *Outline of a Theory of Practice*
Mary Douglas's *Purity and Danger*
Roland Dworkin's *Taking Rights Seriously*
James G. March's *Exploration and Exploitation in Organisational Learning*
Ikujiro Nonaka's *A Dynamic Theory of Organizational Knowledge Creation*
Griselda Pollock's *Vision and Difference*
Amartya Sen's *Inequality Re-Examined*
Susan Sontag's *On Photography*
Yasser Tabbaa's *The Transformation of Islamic Art*
Ludwig von Mises's *Theory of Money and Credit*

Printed in the United States
by Baker & Taylor Publisher Services